GOD IN THE WINDOW

Andrea Lennon

True Vine Ministry

Conway, Arkansas

CONTENTS

✑ Dedication ✑

I dedicate this book to my parents, James and Sandra Morris, my brother, Jason, and my sister, Shannon. You gave me the greatest treasure on earth—a family. I am forever grateful for you and the incredible way God brought us together. He has always been in the window of our lives, directing every step!

PREFACE

As I think about my journey, I can pinpoint several times when God spoke to me and changed my life's direction. The words were not audible, but they were crystal clear. Other times I couldn't see how God was moving in my life; I was just trying to make it from one day to the next. It is only now that I look back and can trace how He brought me from one point to another. I smile when I think about the fact that God shows up in our lives and makes His plan known to us.

Saul, later known as Paul, had a similar testimony. While on his way to Damascus to persecute God's people, God intervened and changed the direction of Saul's life. I'm thankful that my encounters with God have been less invasive than Paul's. (Seriously, I'm so thankful!) However, my journey has been hard at times. I'm sure your journey has had its share of struggles, too.

The pull to live by faith and the pull to be in control have been constant companions to me. I long to be a woman of faith. I can't stand the idea of settling for less than God's best. At the same time, I really want to "call the shots." I really want to stay in the safe and comfortable places where I'm in control. The need to be in control has at times controlled me. It has caused me to run from God instead of running to Him. Without a doubt, the biggest blessing of writing *God in the Window* has been the realization that I need to let go of control and trust God as I daily surrender to His plan.

Maybe you are like me and you like to be in control. If so, I invite you to read my story and learn from it. You don't have to live with the weight of control dragging you down. You can come to a place of peace where you want Jesus more than you want anything else!

Over the years, I have met thousands of women through True Vine Ministry. Women who love Jesus and their families. Women who want to experience God's best in the middle of their ordinary days. Women who are beautiful and gifted. Women just like you. Each story that I have heard and each neck that I have hugged has impacted me. I love teaching the Bible. I love serving women. And I love you. God is so good to let us walk this journey of life and faith together.

All for His glory!

–Andrea

CHAPTER 1

Humble Beginnings

March 11, 1976. For many, it was just another day on the calendar. For me, it was the day I was born. My birth certificate records the following information: I was born at 2:36 p.m. at White County Hospital in Searcy, Arkansas. Doctor Joseph was the attending physician. I was a single birth.

Four facts. That's all I know about my birth. The time, the place, the doctor, and the fact that I was the only one born to my birth mother at that moment. I'm thankful for these four facts. Over the years, I have held on to them and thought, "I know a little about how my life began."

There are so many other things I don't know; facts that are not recorded on my birth certificate. Was my birth mother's labor long or short? Was she alone or surrounded by loved ones? Did she hold me or was I quickly whisked away to the nursery? Did she whisper anything in my ear? Did I look like anyone in my birth family or did my personality favor a certain "someone"? I may never know the answers to these questions, but what I do know is that I love my birth mother deeply, and I'm thankful for the role she played in my life.

Adoption. It's a complex word to me. I love it and grieve about it at the same time. I *love* that my birth mother embraced her role as a mother the moment she gave me a chance at life. I *love* that God placed me in the exact family that He had for me. I *grieve* that I don't know my birth mother. Her name, appearance, and story are a mystery to me. I believe that when you don't know your birth mother or her story, there is a part of your own story that is a mystery to you as well. For me, there is an undeniable connection between a birth mother and her child.

I spent the first four days of my life in the hospital nursery waiting for my adoption to be finalized. Adoption is a beautiful process that has been a long journey of acceptance for me. I spent many years struggling with the unknowns. Who was there? What happened? How did my story begin? When you are adopted, there's a reality you have to face. There are parts of your story others will know that you may never know. I think this fact contributed to my need to be in control of my life. I saw my life as being out of control from the beginning because there were so many things I didn't know.

Have you ever visited a hospital nursery to meet a new baby? You peer in the window and see the babies lined up in bassinets, each one with a name tag identifying who they are and who they belong to. You peer in the window and find that special one you came to see. You smile and talk to them. You beam with excitement when you think about the possibilities that await that small, precious soul.

Who was in my window? That question haunted me for years. *Did I have a name tag? Did anyone come to the hospital to see me?* The likely answers to these questions left me feeling isolated and alone.

In the beginning, another family showed interest in adopting me. I have not met them, and I don't know their story or why things didn't work out. What I do know, and believe deeply, is that God was in control. He had the right family waiting for me! As I was growing in my mother's womb and as I was waiting in the hospital, God was directing the events of my life. He was frustrating the plans that needed to be frustrated, and He was blessing the plans that needed to be blessed.

One day, a couple named James and Sandra Morris drove about two and a half hours from their home in Paris, Arkansas, to Searcy. They stopped by the courthouse to finalize the paperwork and then picked me up from the hospital. It was official: I was theirs and they were mine! That day I got an instant family with an older brother named Jason and a younger sister (born seven short months later) named Shannon.

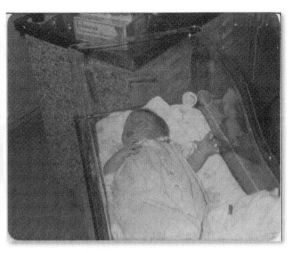

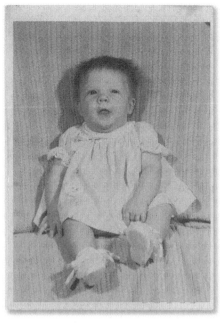

After my parents finalized my adoption, they came to the hospital and picked me up. This picture was taken in the hospital when I was four days old.

My first official baby picture.

My very first room. Mom and dad brought me home from the hospital and this cute room was all mine. When I see this picture, I am thankful for a family and a place to call home.

CHAPTER 2

The Early Years

Life in Paris, Arkansas, was amazing. It was a small, quaint, southern town where everyone knew everyone. Our family lived in a beautiful two-story home on East Academy Street. Jason, Shannon, and I spent plenty of time rolling down the hills in our huge yard. We rode bikes, jumped on the trampoline, swam in the pool, and climbed lots of trees. (We did our fair share of fighting, too!)

Mom and Dad had their hands full with three kids so close in age, especially during the early years. Thankfully, relatives pitched in and helped. Our church also formed a great support network for us. Our family belonged to First Baptist Church, and if the doors were open, we were there.

My parents tell a funny story about me as a three-year-old. It was a Sunday morning, and my parents dropped all the kids off at the church nursery. As soon as Mom and Dad dropped me off, I started to cry. I wanted to go to "Big Church." I cried and cried and cried. Mom and Dad walked away, assuming I would calm down and forget about it. Apparently, I didn't. I cried the entire morning. If that wasn't bad enough, I cried all afternoon and continued to tell my parents that I wanted to go to "Big Church." Thinking they would put an end to my idea, my mom took me back to church that Sunday night. Mom says that I sat perfectly still during "Big Church" and listened to every word. And I never went back to the church nursery.

"Big Church" was a big deal to me. I loved everything about it. The music, the preaching, and the people were so good for me. I was the kid who asked to go to church and was upset if we had to miss a day. I remember sitting in Sunday school class learning about Jesus and the amazing stories in the Bible. Even before I fully understood what it meant to "follow" Jesus, I wanted to. I really did.

Church was my safe place. As soon as I stepped inside the doors, the feelings of anxiety, loneliness, and isolation that constantly seemed to be with me disappeared. I knew I was in a place that was special, and it felt like home to me.

One year, when I was six years old, our church held a revival week. The whole place buzzed with excitement for a month, but I didn't know what to expect until it started. I just knew there would be a week full of fun events and special speakers. We could invite our friends and family and anyone we wanted.

Tuesday night, I learned, was kids night. My parents picked up a van load of kids and took us to church. The fellowship hall seemed enormous that night. It was full of grownups and children, and there were tables lined with hot dogs and potato chips. Everything was grand and wonderful, because I was a little girl in a very special place—my church.

I sat at the back of the room and hung on to every word the preacher said. More clearly than I had ever heard in church or Sunday school, I learned about God's love for me and how He sent Jesus to die for me. I understood about sin and how we all have sin in our lives and how our sin separates us from God. I learned there is nothing we can do by ourselves to get to God, but we don't have to. God made a way when He sent Jesus to die for us. All we have to do is say we are sorry for our sins and ask Jesus to save us. (As a six-year-old, that is what I clearly heard and understood. I love the simplicity of the gospel!)

Then all of the kids moved to join the adults in the sanctuary, where we had the big revival service. The preacher's talk gave me mixed emotions: sadness because of the sin in my life and joy from learning that Jesus had died so I could have a relationship with God. At the end, the preacher said, "If you want to be saved, then come down here to the front of the church."

I was the first one down the aisle. I marched down the aisle with no fear and no shame. I was ready! There were counselors ready and waiting for anyone who wanted to be saved. We went back to the fellowship hall together, and each person who was ready to make a decision was paired with a counselor. I sat at a table with my mom and an older lady from the church, and we talked through what it meant to be saved. I bowed my head and asked Jesus in my own words to come into my heart and save me from my sins. If I didn't know what salvation was about before, I did then. God, through Jesus, gave me a a brand-new life.

Our church took salvation seriously. Before I could be baptized, I had to complete a booklet that went over the basics of the Christian faith. I remember sitting at the dining room table and working hard to complete each chapter. To be honest, I was frustrated. I loved Jesus, and He loved me. I was ready to be baptized and couldn't care less about finishing a booklet!

A few months after my decision to follow Jesus, my mother, sister, brother, and I were baptized at First Baptist Church in Paris. Tears formed in my little eyes as I watched my brother, then my sister, and then my mother declare their love for Jesus. Soon it was my turn. I stepped into the baptistry and had the biggest smile on my face as I was baptized. Even though I was young, the love in my heart for Jesus was real. I knew that I needed Him and that He loved me. In that moment, that was enough.

The more I found that God and His people were a safe place for me, the more I loved them and the more I wanted to go to church. My parents took time and invested in me during my early years. They took me to church and made sure I was where I needed to be to encounter God's love and grace.

First Baptist Church in Paris, Arkansas, was a small church, but God was definitely there with us. When God's presence is in a church, it doesn't matter how many people are in the building or how many resources are available. He changes lives. I'm forever grateful for the people of that small church and the undeniable impact they made on me!

Even as a young girl, I loved a church potluck. Fried chicken was my favorite!

Big brother Jason taking care of Andrea.

Shannon and Andrea with our mom on Mother's Day in 1978.

Shannon, Jason, and Andrea with our dad. This picture makes me feel tired just looking at it!

Granddad Horne and my dad took good care of me. My mom pointed out that both of them had their hands wrapped around me. What an awesome picture of God's love!

CHAPTER 3

Dyslexia

From the very beginning, I struggled to keep up at school. What another student might learn in a day, it would take a week for me to learn. I tried really hard to pay attention because I didn't want to let my teacher down. My kindergarten teacher, Ms. Denton, was tall, thin, beautiful, and had a million-dollar smile. I wanted to be just like her when I grew up. We sat at rectangular tables that were in stations. The ABCs lined the front of the classroom along with a fresh, green chalkboard. Each student had a cubby on the side wall with their name on it. The cubby was special to me because it meant I belonged in that classroom. When I saw that cubby, I knew I had a place.

One day, Ms. Denton handed out the worksheets. "OK, class, I'm going to teach you about the difference between singular and plural. Here's what I want you to do. Cut out the pictures, and then match the pictures with the words that describe them." The pictures were of a dog and several dogs, one table and several tables, one cat and several cats. Our task was simple: Color the picture and glue it next to the word that described it.

I watched as the other students quickly grabbed their scissors and began to cut out the pictures. That was a really easy step for me, too. Then I watched all the students color their pictures to make them look pretty. I wasn't great at coloring, but I could stay in the lines and get it done. But the third and final step was a challenge. I couldn't understand the difference between one dog and a group of dogs. I watched as the other students picked up the glue and put the pictures next to the correct word. I sat there, just wondering what I was supposed to do, mad and sad at the same time. I stared at the pictures and wished I could hide somewhere before I disappointed Ms. Denton.

I've often wondered if that was the very first sign of my learning disability. Even though I didn't know it at the time, I was dyslexic. Dyslexia is a learning disability that is characterized by difficulties with accurate word recognition, poor spelling, and decoding abilities.[1]

---

[1] International Association of Dyslexia, https://dyslexiaida.org/definition-of-dyslexia/, February 7, 2018.

As I struggled in school, the main place where my dyslexia showed up was in my letters. I couldn't tell the difference between the letter "b" and the letter "d." I knew that the letter "b" pointed one direction and the letter "d" pointed the other direction, but I couldn't keep it straight in my mind. It didn't matter how many times I practiced writing my letters; I was constantly mixed up.

Even as a five year old, I looked up to Ms.Denton and wanted to be like her when I grew up. She was a great teacher and always took extra time to help me. Fall of 1981.

Shannon and I were going to a Halloween party with friends in Paris, Arkansas. I am sure mom made us hold hands. October 1980

Jason and I were ready for our first day of school. I was starting first grade.

This was the last time I wore a two piece swimsuit and was so close to a cat. (At least Shannon was holding it.) FYI--- I am not a fan of cats!

CHAPTER 4

"Lord, Prune Me"

I was eight years old, and it was a Sunday night. I was at church, and the pastor was preaching on John 15. He was explaining the picture of God as the gardener, Jesus as the vine, and Christians as the branches. I don't remember everything that was said, but I do remember this statement: "God prunes us. He uses hard times in our lives for a reason. The hard times make us stronger." I knew in that moment that God was speaking to me.

In child-like faith, I bowed my head and prayed, "Lord, prune me." That is all I said. Three simple words. To this day, I think that prayer is one of the most profound prayers I have prayed. God quickly began to answer my prayer. He used my personal shortcomings and challenges to prune and shape me. He also used the challenges others around me faced to reveal His grace in my life.

From the outside, my life looked easy and good. I had the unconditional love of my parents, a solid family structure, a roof over my head, food on the table, clothes on my back, and a ton of opportunities. Yet, somehow my life still felt like a constant struggle.

I grew up with a heaviness in my heart that is hard to describe. The heaviness showed itself in different ways. The most noticeable way was an overwhelming sense of loneliness. Even today, I can be hit with intense loneliness at times. This is crazy to me because my life is full of amazing family and friends.

School was hard for me because I struggled with dyslexia. It was also hard in another way. When I was at school, I was constantly worried that I would do something wrong or fail to do something right. My mom was a teacher at my school, and her classroom was never far. But I felt unsettled most of the time and counted down the hours until it was time to go home.

Back in those days, the principal walked around the school with a paddle in his back pocket to discipline misbehaving children. If a paddling needed to happen, it was done in front of the classroom or in the hallway. This ever-present possibility terrified me! I couldn't stand the thought of myself (or anyone else) getting a paddling. I never received a paddling at school (which is good;I might not have survived!), but when others got one, I probably cried as much or maybe more than they did. I wanted everything and everyone to be OK.

I easily made friends with others, but there were limits I couldn't get past. Whenever I was invited to spend the night at a friend's house or at a birthday sleepover, my entire world came to a screeching halt. A sense of panic would come over me because I couldn't be away from my parents, even for one night. The thought of spending the night at a friend's house or even with a family member made me sick to my stomach. Each time I tried to spend the night somewhere, I had to make the dreaded phone call to be brought home. This went on for years. I made the best I could of the situation and the friendships I had at school and church, but I was sad that sleepovers never worked out.

At the end of my third grade year, we all started looking forward to class picnic day. In a town the size of Paris, it was an epic day. Class picnic day was the long-awaited day when kids played outside, ate all the food they wanted, and simply had fun. The day came toward the end of the school year, and it was a reward for good be- havior as well as a chance to relax and have fun before summer vacation started.

I remember the teachers coming to me and explaining a difficult situation. One of my classmates didn't have a good lunch with her. The teachers asked me to find a way to bring the student to their table and invite her to fix a lunch. It was important, they told me, to not let any of the other kids know what was happening. The teachers didn't want my classmate to feel embarrassed or ashamed.

I remember thinking, "What should I say?" Then the answer came to me, and I ran to the playground. I found her and I said, "The teachers decided to pick one person in the entire grade to come to their table and eat anything they want. And guess what? They picked you!" My classmate smiled, and we ran to the table together.

At first she kept pausing. I don't think she knew what to do with so many choices. I jumped into high gear, grabbed a plate, and started fixing it for her. (I was a Baptist, so I knew what to do with a table full of food!) It was a feast, and I loved watching her enjoy every moment of it.

Later I learned why my classmate was so excited. She showed her original lunch to me, which was a piece of bread with some mold on the corners, a little bit of mustard, and a thin slice of lunch meat. This memory still brings tears to my eyes. I could not (and still cannot) stand the idea of someone not having the basics to survive.

Another memory is from fifth grade. One day a friend of mine looked upset after we received our report cards. I asked him what was wrong. He told me that his report card wasn't good, and he was going to be in big trouble. Although no one wants to bring home a bad report card,

I tried to reassure him that it would be OK. The look on his face told me otherwise.

Then he told me how his dad beat him, and I listened in shock. The details that he shared about previous beatings are still seared in my mind. When he finished, I looked at my friend and told him I was going to pray for him.

I went home from school that day and went straight to my bedroom. I got on my knees, and I began to pray. I stormed the gates of heaven on my friend's behalf!

After a restless night, I quickly got ready for school. As soon as I arrived, I found my friend on the playground. I ran over to him and asked him if he was OK. He looked at me and shrugged, "I'm fine." "But what happened last night?" "Nothing. My dad didn't beat me." I told my friend I had prayed for him. And it hadn't just been any little prayer; I told him I asked God to protect him and to help his dad make good choices. Then I grabbed my friend by his shoulders and looked at him and said, "You can always pray to God, too."

Over the years, I lost track of both of those friends, but I have thought about them many times. I can still see their faces, and I still remember their names. I don't think these encounters happened by accident; God had a reason. Their stories became part of my story. I could have been the one without the food or the one who was beaten, but I wasn't. Through the experiences God put in my life, I learned that my life was hard, but not nearly as hard as it could have been. In the process, God was giving me a love for people and a desire to tell them about His ability to provide and make a way. God was so real during this season of my life, and He kept me so close to Him. That's what happens when He prunes us.

I loved playing softball in Paris, Arkansas. I am on the back row, the first girl from the right.

Book Character Day at Paris Elementary School. Jason was a football player, Shannon was Alice in Wonderland, I was Annie. Mom was dressed up as the Old Lady in the Shoe. My mom deserves a medal for pulling this together!

I was excited to get a Pac Man painted on my face at Frontier's Day in Paris, Arkansas. October 1982.

CHAPTER 5

Step-by-Step

Much of my childhood was defined by my struggle with dyslexia and my struggle to find confidence apart from my parents. Yet in the middle of the hard times, there were plenty of good times. My childhood was also defined by the love of the extended family God had put in my life through the circumstance of my adoption. God was with me each step of the way, and He was filling my life with people whose expressions and actions meant the world to me.

I spent a lot of time with Grandmother and Granddad Horne, my mother's parents. I was always excited to help my grandmother cook or hang the laundry out to dry. I vividly remember her house. Grandmother Horne would give me fifty cents for dusting all the pictures that hung on the wall or were displayed on the shelves in her living room. (Considering how large our family was, that was a good deal for my grandmother!) I watched Grandmother bake cookies, cakes, and pies more times than I can count. We were a good team, and I learned a lot of things by watching her.

My father's mother, Grandmother Morris, was a special lady. She was petite and wonderful. She was easy to be around and loved her family. Going to her house was a treat. She had vintage Coke bottles and more sweets than my parents ever allowed us to eat. Grandmother Morris also tried her best to teach all the "grand-girls" how to crochet. Just for the record, crocheting and dyslexia don't mix!

One year, Grandmother Morris decided to throw a surprise birthday party for me. I'm sure others were in on it, too. All of the kids were told to go to the front living room and play. The door to the kitchen was closed. My Aunt Tooter came in and told all the kids to line up. I found a place at the back of the line as we giggled and jostled in a row. "Andrea, you better get in the front of that line!" said Uncle Buck. I did, and the party waiting for me in the kitchen was amazing! (Yes, I have an Aunt Tooter, and her husband was Uncle Buck. I love how colorful Arkansas names can be!) I remember feeling the love of my family as I walked into the kitchen and saw the cake, party hats, and "Happy Birthday, Andrea," poster.

Growing up, Granddad Horne was my hero. I wanted to be wherever he was, and I was happy doing whatever he wanted me to do. One day Granddad said we needed to work in the garden. We had to till the ground and get it ready for planting season. The garden was large and produced delicious vegetables. All the family members pitched in to work in the garden. Planting, watering, weeding, picking, and canning were all part of the process. Sadly, I didn't inherit a green thumb from my family. These days, my idea of gardening involves a quick trip to Kroger where I visit the "Locally Grown Section" of the store. I'm fine with that!

Granddad told me that my job during the tilling process was to walk behind him and carry a Mason jar of tomato juice. When one of us got thirsty, we could stop and take a drink.

Tilling took time. The purpose of the tiller was to break up and soften the ground so that the seed, after planting, would develop and grow. Granddad and I walked back and forth, back and forth, back and forth, tilling the garden. As we tilled, I noticed that Granddad's boot made a clear mark in the dirt. I watched as Granddad walked behind the tiller and left print, after print, after print. I must have been bored because I decided to make a game out of following Granddad.

I gave Granddad some room, and I started jumping from boot print, to boot print, to boot print, trying my best to keep my small shoe print inside his big boot print. Of course, Granddad's stride was longer than mine. I had to really stretch to make it from print to print, all the while keeping my shoe print inside of his. As I was jumping, I found myself thinking, "This is how I should follow Jesus. I should never get ahead of Him. I should never get too far behind Him. And my little print should never try to overshadow His."

As I jumped from boot print, to boot print, to boot print, I started to sing a song I had learned at church: "Foot-steps of Jesus, that make the pathway glow. We will follow the steps of Jesus wherever they go."

I was happy as could be following my Granddad. I loved him, and I trusted him. On that day, as Granddad and I tilled a physical garden, God was tilling a spiritual garden inside of my heart. God was literally painting a picture of how to follow Him at a practical level. A quiet war started inside of me then. Was I going to be in control, or was I going to accept His control over my life?

Shannon, Jason, and Andrea with Grand-dad Carter and Grandmother Ruby Morris in Nashville, Arkansas. Summer of 1977.

Morris family picture for the First Baptist Church Directory.

The Morris family with Granddad Sam and Grandmother Artie Horne. We had fun celebrating their fiftieth wedding anniversary in December of 1985.

CHAPTER 6

Remedial Classes and Special Education

School got harder and harder for me. It was difficult for me to keep up. By the time I was in second grade, I was struggling. Letters, numbers, sentences, words—everything was jumbled in my head. My dad and mom were so good to me. My dad sat at the kitchen table night after night, week after week, month after month, and helped me learn shortcuts for my letters. I can still hear him saying "A, B, C, D" and using hand motions to point out the direction of the letters.

My mom was a remedial reading teacher, so she had her own tricks to share with me when it came to finding key concepts in a paragraph or reading assignment. She would ask me, "Who is the author talking about? What is the author trying to say?" I'm still amazed at the love and grace of God to place me in a home with two parents who were educators.

Even with all the extra help from my parents, there came a time when my classroom teacher knew I needed help from a specialist. I still have the letter in which my second grade teacher, Ms. Sneed, recommended I go for testing.

December 15,1983

Dear Ms. Foster:

Andrea Morris is a delightful child to have in
my classroom. The anecdotes she has shared with
me show a level of maturity that is above that
of her classmates. She thoroughly enjoys helping other students. The consideration she extends to fellow students is commendable. She
has asked on numerous occasions if there is any
duty in the room she could help with.

Andrea usually tries very hard to complete an
assignment correctly. There are times when she
asks for additional directions because she has
not understood. When a paper is given back to
her, she reacts seriously. She will persevere
until it is done correctly.

Andrea's parents have been very cooperative.
Any communication I've asked for, has always
been returned. Andrea seems to enjoy and love
her family very much. She relates experiences
with her family in an amazingly understanding
way.

Andrea's observations (that she has shared with
Mrs. Trusty and me) about herself make me feel
that she will persevere to succeed.

Mrs. Trusty and I will work with any recommen-
dations given and agreed upon with her parents
to help Andrea in her schoolwork.

Yours Truly,

Mrs. Ann Sneed

So one day my parents took me to a special educational center for academic testing. When my parents introduced me to Cookie, the learning specialist, I liked her immediately. She had a smile on her face, and she seemed to glow from the inside. Cookie was in a wheelchair, but it didn't slow her down. While Cookie had a so-called limiting disability, it didn't limit her. I was fascinated by her can-do attitude as she rolled around the classroom and explained and administered the test.

When we got the results back from the testing, Cookie recommended I go to remedial classes and summer school. My heart sank. I didn't want anyone to know I had a problem. More than that, I didn't want to go to school one second longer than I already had to.

Our Morris family mantra was, "Work hard and do what it takes to get it done." So, I pulled myself up by my bootstraps and started the long journey of remedial classes and summer school. I remained in the regular classroom most of the day. In the afternoon, I walked across the street to the special education building and had small group tutoring on the school campus.

Learning to write in cursive, figuring out shapes for geometry, and typing on a keyboard were challenges that would take years of practice. Reading was difficult because words were confusing to me. If I could read them, they never made sense. Where a normal reader might read a paragraph once or twice for comprehension, I would read it multiple times. I would try to find the key word or key thought so that I could figure out the meaning of the material from that word or thought. I worked hard and tried my best to develop as a reader.

A couple of years passed. I had been to every summer school and tutoring session, and it was time for me to return to Cookie for another round of testing. The results of the test would determine if I had to continue in remedial classes or if I would "graduate" from special education and be able to stay in the regular classroom all day. I hoped and prayed that I could graduate. I was so ready!

I took the test and felt good about my effort. I had tried my best. Several weeks later, my parents met with Cookie and reviewed the test results.

When they came back, I could read the news on their faces. It was clear that I had made progress, but it was not enough. "We talked to Cookie, and she thinks you need one more year of remedial classes," they said. I ran to the bathroom and cried. I felt defeated and wondered if all the hard work would ever make a difference. Thankfully it did. I pushed through one more year of remedial classes and was able to test out of special education. I was so excited to remain in regular classes from that point forward. There were more struggles (and tears) along the way, but eventually I was able to make academic progress.

I constantly "mothered" my dolls and stuffed animals.

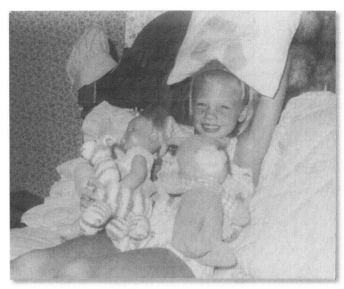

I always dreamed of being a bride! When my older cousin got married, it made my day to put on her wedding dress.

I was a Girl Scout in Paris, Arkansas. I remember working hard to collect the badges.

I never had much rhythm, but I loved to dance as a young girl in Paris, Arkansas.

CHAPTER 7

Moving On

God used a big move and new friendships to teach me about following in His footsteps. When I was in the sixth grade, my dad was offered the executive director position of Twin Lakes Vocational Technical School in Harrison, Arkansas. My parents announced that we were moving to Harrison. When the kids heard the news, you would've thought our lives were over.

I led the charge in overreacting to the move. I remember saying things like, "Our family is going to fall apart!" I hated the idea of change. It was another reminder that I wasn't in control of my life. Paris was familiar to me. I had carved out my spot. I didn't want to start over.

Mom and Dad were patient, but firm; we were moving, and it was going to be OK. We packed up our two-story home and moved to Harrison during the summer between my fifth and sixth grade years. I was awkward and chunky. Acne was beginning to be a problem. The hardest thing to confess is that I had a mullet. (Why?) Sometimes my hair would be straight in the back, and other times I would perm it. Really. It's a painful memory for me. I can't believe no one reached out and helped me with my hair!

Even with all my worries, God was ever faithful. Before we moved to Harrison, I had a dream. In my dream, I met a friend whose name was Amy. The dream was so clear. I woke up and thought, "I wonder if anyone in Harrison is named Amy?" Much to my surprise, there was! Right after we moved to Harrison, we visited First Baptist Church. I nervously walked into a Sunday school classroom that was overrun with boys. There was one girl in the room, and her name was Amy.

Amy Barrett became my best friend. We went to church together, lived in the same neighborhood, and were in the same classes at school. I loved spending time with Amy and her family.

I had played softball in Paris, but the teams were much more competitive in Harrison. I played catcher and was pretty good at it. I was asked to be on the traveling team and enjoyed that for several years. My family was supportive of my desire to play travel ball. It took extra money because of the tournament fees as well as the food, gas, and hotels.

One story stands out from my years of playing softball, and surprisingly, the story has nothing to do with throwing a player out at second base, catching a foul ball off the fence, or talking the umpire into calling a "ball" a strike (all of which happened a time or two).

Our coach called a parents-only meeting. At the meeting, the parents were told that one of our players had recently had a birthday and was technically too old to play on the team. The problem was, she was one of our best players. The parents had to make a decision. Should the team finish the year with the player and risk the chance of being disqualified, or should the team ask the player to step down because of her age? The meeting was long, and lots of ideas were bounced around. Then my dad raised his hand and said, "It matters what we teach our girls. We need to teach them about the "real win" in life—and that means playing hard, being honest, and always following the rules." The decision was made, and the team member was asked to step down. When I heard the story later, I was so proud of my dad for standing up for what he felt was right. Remembering his definition of "the real win" has helped shape the way I live.

School wasn't as hard in Harrison. I was still in one remedial class, but the dyslexic fog began to lift. Words started to make a little more sense. My friends helped me with my homework, and my grades slowly improved. (Slowly!)

In sixth grade, I joined the band (pretty much because my friends decided to join). I was in band all the way through high school, playing the bass clarinet. My true love in the band, though, was the flag line. I tried out in seventh grade and was on the line every year after that.

The youth group at First Baptist Church in Harrison was a Godsend. We had a full-time youth pastor whose job was to pour into our lives. Bible studies, church camp, 5th quarters, DNow weekends: You name it, we did it. Soon after we moved to Harrison, I rededicated my life to Jesus. Although I hadn't turned my back on the Lord or His ways, I knew God was calling me to pursue Him at a deeper level.

Harrison was a great community, and the people were kind and welcoming. I made a lot of friends really quickly and I have many fond memories, but there was one big disadvantage to Harrison as compared to Paris—everyone looked the same. Harrison, both then and now, struggles with no diversity in skin color or cultural backgrounds. Groups who are hostile to people of color make their home there and use the Bible in order to support their beliefs. Even as a young girl, this was hard for me, and I knew it went against the teachings found in the Bible.

My first softball team in Harrison. And the mullet! Why?

The mullet strikes again! This time I was sporting my Central Elementary Challengers sweatshirt. Very fancy for sixth grade picture day!

My softball team in Harrison, Arkansas. I am on the front row, the second girl from the left. This was the beginning of the "awkward years."

CHAPTER 8

The Spiritual Girl

As my spiritual life grew, a few friends and I started meeting to pray once a week at our junior high school. A few more friends showed up, and then word started getting out. Before long, the room was packed, with close to sixty students each week.

Several times, I had the chance to lead friends to faith in Jesus. The girls' bathroom was the usual place where this happened. God was burning a desire in me to tell others about Him.

I'm not sure how it happened or when it happened, but at some point, I started to like the attention I received because of my walk with the Lord. I had found my niche as the "spiritual girl." I was good at something. I was good at "Jesus," and I was good at "Church." I liked the attention I received from adults because of the good choices I made. This need for approval led me to a walk with the Lord that appeared to be all about Him. In the end, it was really all about me. I thought I had it all figured out. I had this "Jesus thing" down. To me, the payoff was that I could control my life. If I did "this" for Jesus, then He would do "that" for me. A perfect partnership. He got my love and devotion; I got His blessing and favor.

I did get genuinely excited when people were saved. But any good thing that happened gave me a sense of security that I was on the right path. Then, when things went wrong, I assumed I was in trouble or hadn't done enough good things. That is the problem with viewing a relationship with Jesus as a partnership; my eyes were constantly on my actions, not on Jesus.

I only listened to Christian music, and Sandi Patty was my favorite. Songs like "Love in any Language," "We Shall Behold Him," and "How Majestic is Your Name" were just a few of the songs I liked. I had every cassette tape that Sandi sold. I would put her tape in my cassette player and try to hit the high notes like a true soprano. I'm sure every dog in my neighborhood howled each time a high-pitched note came from my bedroom!

When I was thirteen years old, my mom heard that the Billy Graham crusade was coming to War Memorial Stadium in Little Rock, Arkansas. Not only was Billy Graham going to preach, Sandi Patty was going to be

51

his special guest! My mom knew how much I loved Sandi, and she knew how much I loved Jesus. I remember hearing her tell my dad, "I think I need to take Andrea to the crusade." When Mom mentioned it to me, I wasn't exactly sure who Billy Graham was, but I was beyond excited to hear Sandi Patty sing live!

On the day of the crusade, we were at my aunt's house in Benton, Arkansas, which was only a thirty-minute drive from Little Rock. My mom asked the other family members if they wanted to go. Eventually, my mom, my cousin, and I got in the car and drove to the stadium. We had gotten off to a late start and the traffic, parking, and walk to the stadium took longer than expected. I remember my mom driving around trying to find a parking space. Because we were late, all the good seats in the stadium were taken. We walked up, up, up to the top of the stadium and finally found seats near the top. It was cold and windy, almost to the point of being uncomfortable, almost to the point of thinking, "I'll be glad when this is over, even though I'm enjoying it."

War Memorial stadium holds around 54,000 people and almost every seat was filled. Imagine the sight of a stadium full of people singing praises to Jesus. It really was a great moment! Sandi Patty hit all the high notes beautifully, Billy Graham preached a powerful message, and hundreds of people responded to Jesus.

I remember the hundreds of people coming down to receive Christ. That moved me. I thought to myself, "I'm watching a miracle take place." That was what captured my heart—the people who were responding to Christ, the people who were being saved in that crusade. I really did love Jesus and wanted others to know Jesus. Not all of my motives were right, but not all of them were wrong.

Fun with friends in the band hall at Harrison High School!

I loved being on the Flag Line at Harrison Junior High and Harrison High School. I am on the back row, the first girl from the left.

Flag Line at Harrison High School in Harrison, Arkansas.

CHAPTER 9

Sitting at The Table

One day when I was in the tenth grade, I noticed in the church bulletin that the women's ministry was offering a summer Bible study for women. The youth group offered a Bible study, and I was involved in one at school, but I wanted more. I just didn't know if teenagers were allowed to join a grown-up study. Nervously, I approached the women's ministry leader at First Baptist Church in Harrison and asked if I could attend the group. She said yes!

My mom and I signed up for the summer study. The study was going to be deep, especially for me. I found out that the leaders had chosen to go through Kay Arthur's Inductive Bible Study on Thessalonians. I bought all of the colored pencils I could find at our local Walmart. I was ready to go!

I did my weekly homework and soaked up the Inductive Bible Study approach. I learned how to look at Scripture and allow God's Word to speak directly to me. I wasn't great at the color-coding method, but the basic concepts helped me learn how to dissect Scripture and get to the heart of a passage.

Often I have been asked, "How did you overcome dyslexia?" I think there are several answers to this question. First, my parents got help for me at an early age. Second, I had teachers that cared deeply about my struggle. Third, I worked hard to learn the techniques that were taught to me. Fourth, and this one excites me so much, I studied God's Word, and I truly believe that the Bible renewed my mind. The Inductive Bible Study approach was a big part of that process.

The women in the summer study invited me to sit at the table with them, both figuratively and literally. They embraced and loved me deeply. I was not someone they "put up" with. No, they took me under their wings and mentored me. My favorite moments were our weekly meetings at different ladies' homes. We would gather, enjoy a fun snack, discuss our lesson, and pray together. I took part in several studies over the next few years. I was committed to Bible study and arranged my school and work schedule around the meeting times.

One day, when I was close to finishing high school, my Bible study group was meeting in a small home in downtown Harrison. The home was quaint, and the group of ladies was small. We were doing one of Kay Arthur's video-based studies (and it was still in the days when videos were recorded on a VHS tape!).

It's funny to me that I can remember every detail from the day. I remember that we had spaghetti for lunch. As we ate, we discussed our lesson. We talked about the sovereignty of God as well as predestination. I was feasting on every word. We moved from the kitchen table to the living room so we could watch the lesson. I sat in a chair and spread my notes and Bible out on my lap. Before long, I moved from the chair to the floor. I wanted to get as close to the television as possible. I knew God was working in my heart in a big way.

As I watched Kay teach, the Lord spoke to me. The voice was not audible, but it was crystal clear. He said, "Andrea, this is what I am preparing you to do." Immediately, I had so many questions. "How am I going to teach the Bible? When am I going to teach the Bible? Who am I going to teach the Bible to?"

Moments of crystal-clear direction from the Lord are surreal and hard to explain. A tightness in my chest that was a mixture of excitement and nervousness washed over me. I didn't know what to think about this call from the Lord.

I didn't tell anyone about this encounter with the Lord for many years. I kept it to myself and tried to figure out what it meant. I could see myself teaching a Sunday school class or maybe a women's Bible study group in a local church, but that was the extent of what I could do. Because of my dyslexia, I had no confidence when it came to reading in front of a group. How could I teach anyone?

Limiting God. That is another area of expertise that I unfortunately have. I tend to look at situations and size them up in terms of what can't happen. Thankfully, the Lord kept speaking clearly to me, sharing His plans even when I thought they were impossible.

Getting ready for prom! Shannon and I had big hair!

Fun at Senior Prom with friends!

Senior Prom with my friend Jonathan.

59

CHAPTER 10

Running and Hiding

High school was a great experience for me. I had a big group of friends who were rock solid. I loved everyone and was able to relate to everyone. I had friends who were "popular" and friends who were not. It didn't matter to me. I was in the band, co-captain of the flag, and elected to homecoming court my senior year. I worked at Family Books and Gifts, which was a locally owned Christian bookstore. I loved my job and viewed it as a chance to serve others.

Just prior to my high school graduation, God, once again, spoke to me about my "call" to ministry. One Sunday night, Pastor Jim Perkins shared a sermon on surrendering to full-time or vocational ministry. The topic seemed irrelevant to me. I was a girl, and from what I had seen, full-time ministry was for men. I was certain that God's plans for me had nothing to do with vocational work (and I had no plans of serving the Lord in full-time ministry!).

As I listened to Pastor Jim speak, a feeling of nervousness and excitement welled up inside of me. I kept dismissing the feeling, though. "I'm a girl, and this message is not for me."

Finally, the sermon was over, and the pastor moved to a time of response. "If God is speaking to you, I want you to come to the front so that the church can pray for you," Pastor Jim said. Immediately, I felt the walls in the sanctuary closing in on me. Long gone were the days of my childhood when I was the first one down the aisle when God called. No. I had a different plan. I knew I would graduate soon, and it was important for me to be in the driver's seat when that happened. I saw graduation as a time to take control of my life and to decide the direction of it.

The congregation stood and sang verse one, verse two, verse three, and verse four of "Just As I Am." I was exhausted by the time we sang the final verse. I was NOT going down that aisle. I was NOT telling my church.

Eventually, the service ended, and I was the first one to leave. I rushed to my car and drove away from the church as fast as I could.

The next week was miserable. I couldn't stop thinking about Pastor Jim's sermon and the way it affected me. I finally thought, "I have to do something about this." I came up with a plan to briefly tell Pastor Jim about God's work in my life. I wouldn't tell him everything; instead, I would keep it simple and to the point. The Lord had stirred my heart during the Sunday-night sermon, and I was willing to admit that much. Nothing more and nothing less.

The following Sunday night, I walked over to Pastor Jim and said, "Last week the Lord did something in my life as you were preaching about call to ministry. I am not sure what He was doing, but I thought you should know." With great seriousness, Pastor Jim looked at me and smiled. He said, "I know, Andrea. The Lord laid that sermon on my heart and told me to preach it for you."

What?! That was not what I wanted to hear. I felt like it was a low blow. Now, the Lord was telling other people about my call to ministry! I was speechless, which didn't happen very often.

Pastor Jim wanted to follow up with a meeting in his office the following day. I agreed to the meeting. I woke up the next morning and found out school was canceled because of snow. I was relieved, thinking our meeting would be canceled, too. It was not. I arrived at the office that afternoon and sat down. I was nervous and not really sure what I was going to say.

The conversation we had that day is a vague memory to me. I told my pastor about my love for the Lord and my love for the Bible. I didn't tell him about my experience during the Kay Arthur VHS tape viewing and how God was calling me to teach women the Bible. I just couldn't bring myself to share something so personal.

What is not vague to me about the meeting that day was my plan as I left Pastor Jim's office. I was going to "pray" about my future and the "call" on my life. This would be the extent of my actions. The type of "praying" I planned to do would never really produce actions. It was more of a nod at God than anything else.

I was so surprised when I was elected to Homecoming Court at Harrison High School in 1993.

My good friend Allen Harris. Allen and I go back many, many years. He is a loyal friend to me and my family.

Homecoming escorts
Jeff and Shane.

This is my favorite picture from High School because it was so spontaneous. What a fun memory with Tim and Allen. I had great friends in High School.

CHAPTER 11

Desert Wandering

I graduated from Harrison High School in May of 1994. I enrolled at North Arkansas Community Technical College in Harrison, affectionately known as "North Ark." My dad was the executive director following a merger between the technical school and the junior college. All three of us Morris kids got our basic education at North Ark. Classes at North Ark were relatively small, and I knew several of the instructors. I lived at home and continued to work at Family Books and Gifts. While my situation looked perfect from the outside, I wasn't excited about staying in Harrison following high school. I wanted to have the "college experience" like many of my friends. I didn't have the best attitude about life in Harrison, post 1994. But there were some good surprises waiting for me.

I transitioned from the youth group to the "College and Career" class at First Baptist following my graduation. The College and Career class thrived. We met on Sunday mornings at church and went out to dinner on Sunday evenings after church. During the week, we met at the leaders' house for a meal and Bible study. It was nice to have some new people in my life.

Despite several hours spent in church each week, my walk with the Lord cooled considerably during this time. Disobedience has a way of doing that. I didn't know it, but I was heading straight into a spiritual desert. There's no doubt that my lack of obedience about ministry as well as my desire to control my life stole the joy of my salvation and caused me to lose spiritual focus. I wanted to be in control and chart the direction of my life. I can look back now and see how God allowed me to have my way.

Joe and Cindy Lennon were the leaders of the College and Career class. They had moved to Arkansas for Joe's job as manager of the Harrison JCPenney store. I had gone to high school with their son, Blake. He was in the same grade as my sister, Shannon, and marched in the band with us. When Joe, Cindy, and Blake moved to Harrison, they bought a home that was one street away from ours. Shannon remembers going to their house and welcoming them to the neighborhood. Before long, the

Lennons joined our church and started teaching the College and Career class. But it wasn't until the summer of 1994 that I found out Blake had an older brother. A tall, dark, and handsome older brother named Jay.

Jay came to the College and Career class because his parents taught it, and the Bible studies took place at their house. I slowly found out a little about his story. He had graduated from Grissom High School in 1988 and enlisted in the Army. After an early release from the Army, Jay enrolled at the University of Alabama in Huntsville. Jay was entering his junior year in college when we met. Like me during this season, Jay was not really that serious about his walk with God. He came to Harrison to be with his family during the summer and attended church because that was expected.

In 1994, our church decided to break with tradition and sing praise choruses along with hymns. Then came the bold decision to use a slide projector instead of hymnals. The projector was placed on a small table next to the front pew. I was involved in the worship ministry, and part of my job was to sit on the front row of the church and advance the slides. It turned out that Jay noticed the "slide girl."

At first, Jay and I were just friends. There was a new coach in town, and I was interested in him. I loved football and thought I would make a great coach's wife. (I was always trying to figure out the next step!) Also, Jay had a unibrow, which was pretty much a deal-breaker for me. (I put unibrows in the same category as mullets;we all have our fashion misses!)

It took the entire summer of 1994 for me to realize I wasn't really interested in the new coach in town. I was interested in Jay, unibrow and all.

At the end of the summer, it was time for Jay to go back to Huntsville. I was surprised when I realized I was sad to see him go. We started writing letters to each other, and after he had been gone a while, a group of us made plans for a road trip to meet Jay in Memphis. It had been a long eight weeks since I last saw Jay. I couldn't wait to see him. Our group of friends loaded a van and made the drive from Harrison to Memphis. Going into the weekend, I wasn't sure if Jay really liked me or not. I knew I liked him. We all spent the weekend together, and it was a done deal. Jay liked me and I liked him!

Communication was going to take work since we were eight hours apart. We wrote letters at least twice a week. The phone bills were high because we talked every night. There was this new thing called "email" I could never figure out, so we stuck with the United States Postal Service. One day, I was waiting on a letter from Jay, and the postman was running late. I waited and waited and waited. Finally, I decided I couldn't wait any longer. I got in my car and tracked the postal work-er down in the neighborhood. It was well worth my ef-fort. I had a letter and a package!

Jay came to Harrison every holiday and during the summers. We met up in Memphis, and his mom and I would visit him in Huntsville. It was hard. Long-distance dating requires a lot of work and pretty much stinks most of the time.

Even with the stress of dating and studies, Jay was as steady as a rock. He didn't get rattled or rushed. We were proof that opposites attract. While I was high-strung, Jay was calm. While I wanted lots of friends, Jay only needed a few. I had a tendency to take on three hundred projects. Jay completed a project before he went on to the next. I knew I loved Jay early in the dating process. He had the ability to ground me, and I needed that.

I didn't tell Jay about my call to ministry. We talked about the Lord and our relationship with the Lord, but we never discussed what we felt God wanted to do with our lives. Like many couples, we assumed we could plan our own lives, and God would bless us as long as we showed up at church and were good people.

One weekend I visited a friend at her college to hang out and have fun. I was looking forward to meeting her friends and seeing what "real" college life was all about. As soon as I got to the campus, I started to cry. I was so embarrassed. We hung out on campus and in her dorm, but I kept going to the bathroom and sobbing. Then I would try to pull myself together and act normal.

Finally, my friend asked me what was wrong. I told her I missed Jay and didn't know how I was going to keep doing the long-distance dating thing. At the time, Jay was home for the summer in Harrison. He was getting ready to return to Huntsville, Alabama, for another year of college. The idea of another year of long-distance dating was too much for me to take.

My friend and I agreed that I needed to get back in my car and drive home to Harrison. I drove straight to Jay's house. He was in the garage working on his motorcycle. As soon as he saw me, he laughed and asked with a smile, "What are you doing here?" I started to cry. "I can't be away from you!"

Jay and I endured one more year of long-distance dating. It was hard, but I knew there was an end in sight. We were engaged that following Thanksgiving and married by summer.

Jay is a gift to me and our family. The qualities that first drew me to him are the same qualities I continue to need in my life. Jay is dedicated, steady, and patient. I am on the go, energetic, and sometimes in over my head. It's funny that the very things that drew us to each other are the very things that can drive us crazy. Still, there is a crazy, good balance in all of it.

Jay and I met, dated, and married while we were both in a spiritual desert. At the very least, neither of us were pursuing Jesus. I, for one, was running from the Lord. Oh, the grace of Jesus! He knew the man for me.

Despite my stubbornness, God was at work, and He was leading the way. He was taking good care of me.

Harrison High School Graduation in 1994.

First Baptist Church in Harrison, Arkansas honored the graduating class of 1994. Notice that Amy Barrett and I were the only girls!

I walked across the stage, got my diploma, and was thrilled! The smile on my face captures the pure joy I felt the day I graduated from High School.

My first public speech was given to a large crowd in May of 1996. I was asked to speak at my graduation from North Arkansas Community Technical College. I was a nervous wreck and the speech was painful for all in attendance.

CHAPTER 12

Stormy Beginnings

Jay and I were married on June 1, 1996. I woke up that morning to a loud clap of thunder and a bright bolt of lightning. I put my head under the pillow and thought, "Please, not on my wedding day!" By the time my sister, mom, and I went to the salon, there was an absolute downpour. It was the kind of rain that made you look for animals because you knew that they were, once again, lining up two by two. Because of the rain, my hair wouldn't hold a curl, which made me cry. This made my makeup run. It wasn't how I planned my wedding day.

Thankfully, the sun came out just in time for the ceremony. Curl or no curl, it was a beautiful day.

I look back on the pictures from the wedding and think, "I was just a baby!" I had just turned twenty years old. Jay was twenty-six years old. I can't believe my mom and dad let me get married so young! (Not that they could've stopped me; I was IN LOVE and had life FIGURED OUT!)

Jay and I went on a cruise for our honeymoon. As we were on the cruise, I had a growing sense of anxiety in my heart. I knew that I was moving as soon as we returned to the United States. Jay had assured me that we would only stay in Alabama long enough for him to finish his marketing degree. I was counting on it! I also secretly wondered if the fear of being away from my parents would surface again. I had developed into an independent person, but I had never lived in a different state from my family.

Bottom line: I wasn't looking forward to the move. I was an Arkansas girl, and I really liked the safety of my friends and family in northwest Arkansas. I never really thought about the move until I was packing my car. I'm sure my mom and dad had a kindhearted laugh at my expense. It was time for me to grow up, and it was going to be a long process.

Jay and I drove separate cars to Huntsville. I had a maroon Oldsmobile that practically screamed "old lady." I cried for most of the drive. As we approached Alabama, I decided to turn on the radio. I hit the scan button and found a Christian radio station. Immediately, I stopped crying and started worshipping. Even though my heart was far from the Lord, there was something sweet about singing praises to His Name. I was reminded that God loved me and that He was with me.

We arrived to the apartment, which was located in a very affordable part of Huntsville. (This is a nice way of saying, "Oh, my word, it was a dump!")

Once we settled in, I needed to find a job. I went to the mall and talked to the manager of the Christian book-store. He asked to meet with me at the food court and, following a brief conversation, I was hired on the spot. Since I had worked at a Christian bookstore in Harrison and thrived in that job, it made sense to try to find a similar job in Huntsville.

Jay began his final year of school and also found a job in the alumni office at the university. Married life was different from my dream of "happily ever after." I have to admit that the first year of marriage wasn't fun. Jay and I had never really been around each other for long periods of time. Now, all of a sudden, Jay was the only person I saw. We were together 24/7. Our time together was very different from dating life. Dating was *movies* and *popcorn* and *dinner* and *long talks* and *butterflies in my stomach*. Marriage was *laundry* and *bills* and *Hamburger Helper* and *five dollars until payday*. Talk about a hard-core dose of reality!

One of the few highlights of our week was attending a great church in Huntsville, where we joined the young couples' Sunday school class. We never really made friends at the church, but the music and the preaching were more progressive than my church in Harrison. Southside Baptist Church was on fire for Jesus. God was at work in my heart even if I didn't know it. I was wrestling with God. I was wrestling with my calling. I still hadn't told Jay anything about my calling, so I felt very alone. I remember longing for God; yet, I was unwilling to give up control of my life. God was graciously allowing me to experience the full weight of my disobedience. He is good like that. Although He doesn't force Himself or His plans on us, He never gives up on us.

Jay had friends in Alabama, but it was hard for me to find a place to fit in. For the first time in my life, I wasn't surrounded by friends. I didn't really have a safety net of people to look to for acceptance. Even though I never let friends get too close, I was used to having lots of "peeps" around me. But that was before I was lost in the sea of people known as Alabama. One day I remember thinking, "Maybe I should go back home. Maybe this marriage and move were a mistake."

I turned to food as my friend. We didn't have much money, so we ate cheap food that was full of empty calories. Pasta was a staple for us. Spaghetti, pigs in a blanket, tacos—if we could buy it for less than five dollars, it was on the menu. I gained forty pounds. And I cut my hair really short. It was not a pretty sight! I can't imagine what Jay was thinking during that first year!

One day I was at home because it was my day off from work. Jay was working at the university. Since I didn't know anyone in Huntsville, I stayed home on my day off and cleaned the apartment or watched television. Suddenly, there was a knock at the door. It startled me, but I didn't think too much about it. Figuring it was a door-to-door salesperson, I went to the bedroom and pretended I was not home. Then I heard someone trying to break in to the apartment. I was terrified. My mind was racing. I knew there was a gun in the apartment, but I did not know how to "work" it.

Thankfully, we had a front and back door to our second-floor apartment. I grabbed my purse and keys and ran out the back door. I drove around to the front of the apartment and saw a man hiding in the bushes. I didn't have a cell phone and didn't know what to do. I drove to the university and went to Jay's office. It was at that moment that I realized I was still wearing my pajamas. (And, of course, no bra!) The people at Jay's office were so nice and let Jay come home to check the apartment. They also excused my lack of proper clothing!

From that point on, my goal was to get out of Huntsville and back to Arkansas. I didn't stay at the apartment alone and even invited a young lady who I met through my job to stay with us on our couch for a few months while her husband served overseas. I didn't want to be alone, and I was desperate to fill my life with people and meaning.

Jay's graduation was approaching, and he needed a job. We both wanted to return to Arkansas, but all of Jay's contacts were in Alabama. I remember the day he came home from school and told me that his professor wanted to recommend him for a job in the Huntsville area. My heart sank. "I'm going to live in this sea of loneliness forever!" At the same time, I wanted to be supportive, so I put on a good face. I told him I was "with him," so he should proceed with the interview. Jay went to the interview, and I paced the floor in our small apartment. When Jay came home, he said it wasn't the job for him. I hid the happy dance that was going on inside of me.

Jay made a few calls to companies in Arkansas. He set up three interviews that would take place over the course of three days. One was in Conway. One was in Harrison. And one was in Springdale. I didn't necessarily want to move back to Harrison, but I was open to anything in Arkansas.

I stayed in Huntsville to work while Jay drove to Arkansas for his interviews. The first stop was Conway. Acxiom Corporation was a database company with several entry-level job openings. Jay had an interview with a team of people. He left the interview and called me. He felt good about it. However, he was keeping his options open. He was really excited about the idea of northwest Arkansas.

Jay spent the night in Conway and planned to wake up early the next morning and drive to Harrison. He went to sleep that night feeling pretty good about his options.

When he woke up the next morning, the state of Arkansas was shut down. An ice storm had hit the state, and all Jay could do was wait it out in his hotel room.

Later that day, the folks from Acxiom called Jay. Drum roll ... they offered him a job. Jay called to tell me the news. I asked him how much did it pay. Jay said a number that seemed unbelievable: "TWENTY TWO THOUSAND DOLLARS for the year." I thought, "We are going to be rich!" I screamed into the phone, "Take it!"

The other interviews were canceled. Jay slipped and slid back to Huntsville. I think he got a speeding ticket on the way home, but we didn't care. We had a job, and we were moving to Arkansas. Life was heading in the right direction.

We didn't have much furniture to move, but we did our best to pack our bags and boxes. Jay and I drove out of Huntsville during a rain and hail storm. Tornado sirens were blaring. It was a fitting end to what felt like a stormy season of life.

Our engagement picture!

Jay and I at our wedding rehearsal. Shannon
was my maid of honor and Blake was Jay's
best man.

Shannon and I fixed Jay's collar a few hours before the wedding!

Our wedding day on June 1, 1996. It was raining outside, but the love in our hearts was more than enough to make the day just right.

I was a young bride, but so happy to be getting married. A friend asked me, "Are you nervous?" I said, "No!"

CHAPTER 13

Returning Home

Conway is located in the heart of Arkansas, thirty minutes north of the capital city of Little Rock. Growing up in Arkansas, Conway was always a place we drove through. We drove through Conway to get to Little Rock. We drove through Conway to get to my grandmother's house in south Arkansas. My parents drove through Conway on the day they brought me home from the hospital. And then one day, Jay and I drove to Conway and stayed. Thanks to Jay's new job, it wasn't a passing-through place anymore.

Conway is a unique and wonderful city. Although the population is only 65,000, the city has one university and two colleges. During the school year, the city floods with over fourteen thousand students from around our nation and world. Conway is smart, young, professional, and maintains a great small-town atmosphere while providing a neat and diverse place that is full of opportunities.

I had promised my parents I would finish my education, so I decided to enroll at the University of Central Arkansas (UCA). The two-year degree I received from North Arkansas transferred, so I started as a junior.

When we moved to Conway, we were ready to settle into life there. We were excited about being back in Arkansas and being close to our family. And we were looking forward to making friends. Huntsville had been like a nine-month drought for me in regard to friendships and relationships. Looking at our future, I decided I was going to conquer Conway. Conway would be a place that I loved, and Conway would love me!

I developed this plan to help gauge our friendship development in Conway. Before I tell you the plan, take a deep breath and know that my control issues were deep, and they touched every single area of my life.

The first stage of the friendship process was that Jay and I were going to discover places to go and things to do. We did that for several months, and it was a lot of fun. We loved exploring Conway, and we loved exploring central Arkansas. We just settled into that first phase of finding things to do and going different places, and we didn't rush it. We also went home to Harrison pretty often, so we were able to spend time with family and friends in northwest Arkansas.

Then we moved into stage two, which was a little more exciting. Stage two meant we were going to the fun places, and while we were there, we were seeing people we knew. Since we were actively trying to make friends, we were meeting people and sizing them up as possible friend prospects. Maybe the people would be from church, or from the community, or Jay's job, or my classes at UCA. Stage two meant we were making progress because we were connecting with people.

But that was not the end of the story. I had a third stage, and that is where everything in my mind was pointing. I wanted to go to the fun places WITH the people we knew. That was success to me! Going places with our new friends meant I finally had my dream life where I was loved and wanted—where I had a place to belong.

The beginning of our time in Conway was all about finding friends, establishing a life, establishing relationships, and following the three-stage friend process. I remember walking Jay through the process and charting our progress along the way. He just kind of looked at me and nodded his head. I am sure he was rolling his eyes in his mind but seeing me happy was probably a relief for him.

I worked for a plastic surgeon while attending UCA. I was the receptionist and filed insurance. I wasn't on the cutting edge of style or fashion, which made that job choice a little unusual. Jay was a trooper; I wasn't in good shape, and my hairstyle was cringeworthy. I felt homely. My big "fashion-forward" move was to get blonde highlights from time to time.

Working for a plastic surgeon was eye-opening on many levels. Not all of the cases were cosmetic. Many of the cases were incredibly moving and inspirational. Burn patients, cleft palates, and injuries from accidents were common. We saw it all. Some women came in chasing beauty. My heart always connected with these ladies. Jay and I didn't have the money for cosmetic procedures, and it wasn't who I was, but I could identify with the struggle to try to gain value from your appearance.

My job was to welcome the patient and ask them to fill out their paperwork. I got to know many of them and tried not to wince when I heard about some of the uncomfortable procedures they wanted. I didn't like for anyone to be in pain, even if the pain was from their own choices. I tried my best to stay away from the patient rooms—and any dramatic noises.

One day I heard a loud noise coming from the back of the office. My mind was racing with all the possibilities. Was that the sound of liposuction or laser hair removal or something worse? I had no idea!

The doctor came out from the back, and I must have been as white as a ghost. He looked at me and asked if I was OK. I said, "What in the world were you doing back there?" I braced myself for the answer. With a smile on his face and a cup of coffee in his hand, he said, "Making a cappuccino." It was at that moment that I knew my empathy levels were on steroids!

When I enrolled for classes at UCA, one of the first things I had to do was pick a major. My parents encouraged me to think about education, which made sense. A teaching degree allows you to have a family-friendly schedule, and teachers are needed everywhere so there are lots of opportunities. The only problem was that I didn't want to be a teacher. The same heaviness I felt during elementary school came over me every time I thought about teaching. I didn't enjoy my days in school, and I couldn't picture myself working at a school.

In my mind, teachers needed to have neat handwriting, good spelling, and be strong readers. I wasn't great at any of those things. So, I decided to take a very practical approach to picking a degree. I opened the University of Central Arkansas catalog, and I started on page one, thinking, *"Surely this university offers something I can do."* I remember flipping from page to page, hoping something would jump off the page and scream, "Pick me!"

God had clearly called me to serve in ministry. I was supposed to teach women the Bible. He had shared His plan with me time and time again. I ran from His plan because I thought mine was better. I ran from His plan because I thought I could create something that was safe and doable. I ran from His plan because I knew I couldn't do what He was calling me to do. I ran from His plan because I wanted to be in control.

Instead of helping me, running landed me in a place of total confusion. It landed me in a place of picking my major by opening a catalog and trying to find something that made sense. Something that was manageable or doable based on my abilities and resources. Whether I realized it or not, I was attempting to find my purpose and direction in a college catalog.

As I flipped through, I saw Family and Consumer Science (FACS), also known as Home Economics. I thought, "I can do that. I like to cook, and I like to eat." I read a little further. "I can't sew, but I can wing that one."

The FACS program offered different degree plans: interior design, nutrition, and education. I was relieved when I saw that one of the degree plans was in the field of education. Perfect! Even though I didn't want to be a teacher, I could get a degree in education, and it would buy me some time until I figured out what I wanted to do with my life.

I started classes and liked them, but my days of wanting to be a "normal" college kid were over. I didn't join any organizations or groups. I came to school for class and left as soon as I was done.

Jay and I joined a church in Conway and made some great friends who became like family to us. We worked with the youth, and I sang on the praise team. Life was good, but something was missing. Looking back, it wasn't something, but Someone. Jesus wasn't at the center of our lives.

We went to church, but we were really chasing the American dream. I wanted a big house, nice cars, a couple of kids, and a bank account that would fund our dreams. Anything else was failure to me. During this time, I didn't read my Bible. I may have prayed from time to time, but it was probably nothing more than, "Lord, bless this," or "Lord, do that," prayers. I was trying to make life work on my own.

I was pretty naïve, too. When Jay and I decided to buy a home, I was drawn to some large, beautiful ones. When I showed them to Jay, he constantly said, "We can't afford that home." Finally, I asked, "Why not?" "Honey, the payment will be too high." I looked at Jay and said, "I don't think that's how it works. We can just tell the bank how much we want to pay." (Not even kidding!)

Conway was booming, and new homes were being built. There were lots of starter homes that were reasonably priced. We decided to buy a home in a brand-new subdivision. We picked out a lot and a house plan. We watched our small home take shape. I was able to pick out the wallpaper, carpet, and paint colors. I loved our little home. I think it was around 1,200 square feet. We made the most of every inch. I thought, "Maybe this is the path to the American dream!"

I was nearing the end of my degree plan at the University of Central Arkansas, and the hardest part was yet to come. I had to complete a full semester of student teaching. The thought of it made me feel sick at my stomach. The closer I got to student teaching, the more miserable I became. The same heaviness that I felt with school in my elementary days was back.

I remember driving to my first teaching assignment and helping the sweet teacher set up her classroom. She was precious, and you could tell that teaching was a calling for her. She literally thrived in the classroom. I loved seeing this in her life, but it was hard for me, too. I didn't feel that way about teaching, and I knew I couldn't hide it. I came home from that first day of teacher meetings and had the longest and hardest "cry" of my life. I sobbed at the state of my life. How had I lost my way?

When I returned to Arkansas, I thought all of my problems would be solved. I had been so sure that being "home" and having friends would fill the void in my life. I was wrong.

CHAPTER 14

Only Jesus

Soon Jay and I found ourselves looking for a new church. We had slipped into the "consumer Christian" mindset. We had our list of ideals. The music had to be just right; the sermon needed to be on point. We visited lots of churches in Conway, but nothing ever seemed to "click" with what WE wanted and what WE liked.

Jay had a colleague named Casey. Casey was persistent (and I do mean persistent) in inviting us to Second Baptist Church. We had visited Second Baptist when we first moved to Conway and had marked it off our list.

Casey wouldn't take no for an answer. Finally, we agreed to visit Second Baptist again. We met some friends on our first visit, and they wouldn't let go of us. Looking back, it was a beautiful thing. We didn't stand a chance! Before long, we were attending each week and even joined the young couples class. God quickly knitted our hearts with the people of Second Baptist Church, and they became family to us.

The Women's Ministry of Second Baptist offered the study, *Jesus the One and Only* by Beth Moore. All the girls from the young married class decided to sign up and attend together. It had been years since I had been in an organized women's Bible study. My memories of Kay Arthur and her Inductive Bible Study were fuzzy at best.

The Beth Moore Bible study was full of homework and asked for a lot of time every week. But somehow that was not a hard commitment for me. If anyone had asked what was happening to me during that study, I would have said, "I'm falling in love with Jesus. He is sweeping me off my feet!"

Like with the Kay Arthur studies, one of the highlights was meeting up with other women each Wednesday night. We came to the church, checked in at the registration table, helped ourselves to a treat from Maggie's Cookies, and found our spot at the table. We laughed and learned together. Every time, I left refreshed and energized. As I drove home after each study, I would voice the same thought inside of my heart: "Where have you been, Lord?" His gentle reply to my soul was always the same: "I've been here all along." I was so drawn to the Lord and to His Word and to His people. I had been running for so long, but the grace of God had caught me and wouldn't let me go. I was tired of trying to figure out life on my own, and I really wanted Jesus in my life. I needed Him. I wanted Him. I knew in my heart that I loved Him, and He loved me.

Sometimes I say that God is sneaky. I mean this with total respect to our Lord. This was one of those moments in my life. I didn't realize it at the time, but God was placing me in the exact environment that I had run from several years prior.

One week, I was asked to lead the Bible study. I was nervous and excited at the same time. I'm sure I over-prepared. The forty-five minutes that we spent in God's Word were absolutely amazing, like a cold drink of water on a hot summer day.

I started to feel a deep hunger for the Bible again. I even started praying on a regular basis. Everything was so fresh and so new. Jesus drew me to Himself, and though I probably would have run the other direction had I known all that was ahead of me, I couldn't. I knew I needed Jesus, only Jesus. I had been searching for happiness in the American dream, with new friends and a new home. Thankfully, Jesus didn't allow me to settle for a temporary home. He was calling me to return home ... to Him.

These sweet friends were in our newly wed class at Second Baptist Church in Conway, Arkansas. They loved us and wouldn't let us go. Such a sweet gift from our Lord! (Front row: Richelle, April, Felicia, Melinda. Back row: Andrea, Melissa, Sherri, and Robyn)

CHAPTER 15

Jake

Naïve or not, I approached having children with the same determination that I approached moving to Conway or finding a house. How complicated could it be? When a couple wanted to get pregnant, they would get pregnant, and then they would have the baby, and then they would raise the baby, and then everything would work out! It would be like a formula.

I thought, "This is great, we're now at the season of life when we're ready to have a baby." So we started trying. Nothing happened. We didn't wait for years and years like many couples face, but we went through six to eight months of nothing. When I went to the doctor, he said, "That's normal. Try for another year. If you're still having trouble after that, come back."

I thought, "Oh my goodness, a whole year of just trying? That's not the plan. This child was already supposed to be one at that point!" God was definitely teaching me. Jay and I continued to try, and I did conceive and was so excited. I remember taking the pregnancy test and running into the living room and showing Jay. From the moment the test turned blue, I was so sick. Sick, sick, sick. Which was a good sign, although it was just miserable.

I made an appointment with my doctor and filled out all the necessary paperwork. We had already told everybody we were expecting. When we went in for that first appointment, the doctor couldn't find a heartbeat. My own heart sank, and I was terrified. I thought, "Andrea, you have told the ENTIRE WORLD that you're pregnant, and what if you're not?" The doctor told us, "You're probably fine; it's probably just really early in the pregnancy. The fact that you're sick is a good sign." Of course, I was thinking, "I'm probably making all of this pregnancy up in my head! I'm just crazy!"

I called my parents, I called my close friends, and I asked everybody to pray. The next day, we went to the hospital for an internal ultrasound. As soon as we got to the exam room, they picked up the heartbeat. "It's a strong heartbeat. Everything's fine," they told us. I was so relieved.

I found out I was pregnant during the last six weeks of student teaching. Thankfully, I was teaching at a school in Conway. The only thing that tasted good to me was the Tuna Pita Sandwich and a large water with lemon from a favorite local restaurant called Stoby's. I had developed a huge food aversion to chicken. I couldn't look at it, smell it, or even be around people when they talked about it.

Other moms described pregnancies and feelings of bliss. For me, it was like an alien invasion. I threw up every single day for almost forty weeks! I gained fifty pounds. Jake kicked and moved constantly. It was as if a three-ring circus was going on inside of me.

Somehow, I made it through the final few weeks of student teaching and walked across the stage of the University of Central Arkansas, hoping I wouldn't throw up as I received my diploma.

My pregnancy turned out to have been well-timed as far as my teaching career went. Jay and I agreed I should stay at home once the baby was born. I received several teaching offers and was delighted to have an excuse to turn them down.

The Sunday before the baby was born, I decided it would probably be my last kid-free day so I laid out by our friend's swimming pool all day long. I proceeded to get the worst sunburn of my life. Thirty-eight weeks pregnant and sunburned from top to bottom. Miserable, I slathered aloe vera all over my sunburned body.

That night, my sister came to Conway to spend the night and help us get the nursery ready. I was sunburned and not feeling well in general, but I wasn't due for two more weeks. Shannon made it in time for dinner, and the NBA Finals were on television. My lower back was hurting, and I had cramps in my stomach. Still, we talked about what we would do for the nursery until I couldn't pay attention any more.

Shannon started timing the "cramps," and finally she told us they were coming every seven minutes. Jay and I had no idea what labor felt or looked like. We started reading every book and pamphlet we had picked up. We discussed going to the hospital, just in case, but Jay reminded me that we would just have to drive back home again if it was false labor.

Finally, Jay decided to go to bed. I decided to sleep on the couch since I couldn't get comfortable. I made it thirty minutes before I woke Jay up. I told him I was going to the hospital, and he could come along if he wanted. (I was a little edgy!) He did. We left Shannon at the house, figuring we might be back soon. As we drove, we debated whether I was in labor or not. I told him, "If this is not labor, I quit!"

We arrived at the emergency room of Conway Regional Hospital, but I was soon sent to labor and delivery. We were shocked to learn that I was in active labor, already dilated to six centimeters. And all that aloe vera I had smeared on my sunburn meant the nurses couldn't get any of the monitoring equipment to stick on me! Not the heart monitor, not anything. They had to keep swiping it away as I labored, but in the end, it didn't matter.

Jake Carter Lennon was born on June 15, 2000, at 1:10 a.m. He weighed 6 pounds and 15 ounces. We were in love! He was strong and independent from the very beginning and didn't want to be swaddled. He loved to kick his arms and legs. Because his birth happened in the middle of the night and because it was two weeks early and so unexpected, it was just me, Jay, and Jake at the hospital. For us to have that sweet time, just the three of us, was very special. It's one of the things I loved about Jake's birth, compared with my own birth. By 9:00 the next morning, the floodgates opened, and family and friends came pouring in. We had the best day welcoming Jake to this world.

When Jake was born, the hospital had a policy where the baby "roomed in" with the parents. This meant that the baby stayed in the room with you all of the time. I loved having Jake in the room with me, but memories of my own birth came to mind. I remembered the nursery window and how I wondered if anyone looked through the window at me. I hit the call button and asked the nurse to come and get Jake and take him to the nursery. She agreed. I walked down the hallway to the nursery and peered in the window. I remember telling him, "I see you! You are mine! I will love you forever!"

When it was time for us to leave the hospital, I panicked. "I can't believe they're going to let us walk out of here with this baby! Do they know if we're responsible? If we are ready? Is there not a checks-and-balance system?" It was like, "Welcome to the real world. You are a parent."

Even with my lack of experience, or maybe because of it, I threw myself into parenting Jake. It was as though he was my new project.

Jake was the object of my attention. I loved him deeply and was so excited to be a mom. I had dreamed of being a mom my entire life! However, I hadn't fully dealt with issues from my past or with my own struggles with control, so I made a lot of mistakes because of that. I remember that my goal for Jake was to make him into a great person. He was someone for me to shape, mold, and put all of my energy into to achieve this great person. I made a lot of mistakes because of that. I didn't let Jake have his individuality the way I would if I were to do it again. Of course, I was in my twenties then, and I'm in my forties now. Parenting is a process that allows us to learn, grow, and mature.

I wanted Jake to be a perfect baby, so we followed all the rules. He was put on a feeding schedule and a sleeping schedule and a playtime schedule. Everything followed a routine. Jake adapted and did well; however, he would never be a strict rule follower, even if I tried to make him one!

Jake's first birthday party!

Graduation from the University of Central Arkansas. I was pregnant with Jake and trying hard to smile. I was so sick!

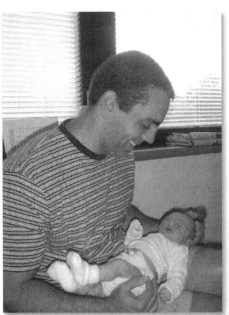

Proud dad! Jake was a few hours old.

Jake was a busy little boy. He kept me on my toes!

Jake was a happy baby. He always had a smile on his face.

Chapter 16

Promises, Promises

Jake was one year old. I had been faithfully studying my Bible and praying. Beth Moore was scheduled to host a Living Proof Live event at the Pyramid Arena in Memphis, Tennessee. One of my high school friends was living there and invited me to join her and her mom for the weekend. I agreed, excited to have my first weekend away since Jake was born.

In the weeks leading up to the event, I told Jay, "God is doing something. I just can't put my finger on it. We had better be ready."

Jay knew nothing about my call to ministry. It never came up in conversation before or during our marriage. In fact, I had forgotten about it. I never thought about it, or the Kay Arthur videotape moment, or the sermon that my pastor in Harrison preached on that Sunday night about vocational ministry. All of those things were long gone from my memory. If I remembered my call to ministry at all, I would have assumed I made it up in my head. Or that I had missed my chance. I wasn't still so naïve as to think only men could do ministry, but I was a housewife and stay-at-home mom. Obviously, I wasn't in a place where I could do anything for God. So much had happened in my life since my teenage years of studying the Bible. So much time had passed.

When the day of the Beth Moore event came, I remember riding in the car and thinking, "When I leave this conference, I will not be the same." I had already attended lots of conferences by then, and I've attended lots since. The sure feeling that God was going to move in my life has never equaled that experience.

As we approached the Pyramid, I bowed my head and my heart. I remember saying, "Lord, whatever you tell me to do, I will do it." We walked inside and found seats. When the event started, Beth took the stage and posed the question, "What if the heart changed?" I thought about the question and asked myself, "What if my heart really did change? What would my life be like?" Then Beth shared that a nurse had told her the symbol for change is a pyramid. Her point was clear: God was ready to change hearts. He was ready to change lives. I knew the Lord was speaking to me.

I am a "Type A" girl who loves to make a list. (Sometimes I make a list of things I have already done just so I can mark them off.) That night at the Pyramid, I decided to make a list of all the things God told me. I wanted a tangible list of things to do or not to do. I started writing. "Begin each day on my knees." "Pray before I respond."

Then it happened. I can't explain why or how, but it happened. I wrote, "Look into seminary." I read the phrase on my own list and thought, "WHAT IN THE WORLD?!" I had never wanted to go to seminary, but more than that, I don't think I had even spoken the word seminary out loud. Ever. Not one time in my entire life!

Immediately, I tried to break the promise I made in the car. The Lord was certainly putting my heart to the test. The promise of "I'll do whatever you tell me to do" was no longer the cry of my heart. I began to talk to the Lord. "Oh, Lord, I can't do that. I am a wife. I am a mother. I am a GIRL!" (As if the Creator of the universe, Who made me, didn't know the specifics of my life!)

The Lord spoke quietly and briefly to my soul. His voice was not audible, but it was crystal clear. He asked a question: "Do you not think that I am big enough to do all of that in your life?" I let out a long sigh and resolved to "look into" seminary.

I called Jay that night, and I told him we needed to talk. He says he still remembers the conversation. I said, "Jay, the Lord told me that I need to look into seminary. I don't know why, but I think we are OK. He just said that I have to 'look.' I don't think I actually have to go …"

Once I was home, I got online and looked at all the major Baptist seminaries. Not one of them would be a good match for me or my family. I found that all of them were too far away from our house and Jay's job. Relieved, I decided that I had done what God said to do. I had "looked into" seminary and obviously the option was not for me.

Not long after, I chatted at church with our minister of education, Freddie Pike. I mentioned to him that I had been looking at seminaries, but they were all too far away for me to register. "Andrea," he said, "Did you know that Southwestern Baptist Theological Seminary has an extension campus in Little Rock?" SWBTS is based in Fort Worth, Texas, about six hours away from Conway. But Little Rock, the capital of Arkansas, was only thirty minutes away. A look of fear must have washed over my face, as I admitted I hadn't known that. Freddie smiled. "You should look into it."

I got back on the SWBTS website and discovered the information about the extension campuses. Then I decided I could at least "look at" the admissions process. In my heart, though, I believed there was no way I would qualify for seminary.

The admissions representative was very helpful. She answered all the questions I could think to ask. But she did mention one problem. "Since it's late summer, it will be hard for you to complete the admissions process and be registered in time for the fall semester." "Perfect!" I thought.

Jay and I agreed that I should fill out the admissions packet anyway. We wanted to be able to say that we thoroughly "looked into" seminary even though I never intended to go. Since the admissions representative thought the timeline wouldn't work out, filling out the packet seemed like a safe step. I gathered all of the requested information, requested college transcripts, and filled out the questionnaires and forms. When it came to gathering character references, though, I was stuck.

SWBTS required a reference from your pastor or a staff member at your local church. During my application process, our church called a new pastor, Mark Dance. Mark and Janet moved to Conway from Tennessee. I went back and forth on the decision to ask Mark for a reference. It was difficult for me to go to someone I didn't know and ask them to recommend me for something I knew I could never do. In the end, I decided to reach out to Mark. He agreed to meet with me and consider making the recommendation. What I have never told anyone is that I was so nervous about my meeting with Mark. I wondered if he would give me some kind of seminary aptitude test. I wanted to be prepared, so I practiced saying all the books of the Bible and made sure I could list all of the disciples in the New Testament. Of course, anyone who knows Mark would laugh at the thought of him giving me a test! Mark and Janet are laid back and easygoing. They are the least "churchy" people I know. That is just one of the reasons I love both of them!

My meeting went surprisingly well, and I was relieved when Mark just asked questions about my faith and experiences, instead of quizzing me. In the end, he agreed to send in a reference. I gathered the rest of my references and paperwork. I put everything in the mail and thought, "Surely that is enough. I've been obedient. I've 'looked into' seminary."

I turned in my application and enjoyed the next few weeks of life. I felt like I had done my part. Now, I could get back to raising Jake and volunteering at church. One day in early August, I went to the mailbox and saw an envelope from SWBTS. I opened the letter and was shocked to read the first line: "Congratulations, you have been accepted to Southwestern Baptist Theological Seminary ... ." I felt like collapsing onto the floor. "What does this mean? What am I going to do? When did I lose control of my life?" I wondered.

I decided to wait until Jay came home from work to show the letter to him. The (crazy) question, "Should I go to seminary?" kept running through my mind. Jay came home, and we talked. We discussed what we would need for me to go to school. The first need was money. We needed $1,200—in the next few weeks—in order to pay for the fall semester. The second need was childcare. The extension classes in Little Rock met all day on Monday. This meant we would need to find a place one day a week for Jake to go.

Both seemed like impossible obstacles. Once again, I was relieved about the possibility of things NOT working out. At the same time, I was a little nervous and excited. Jay and I spent a lot of time asking God to show us the way. Our parents knew about the process and encouraged us while we waited.

We went to Second Baptist that next Sunday, still full of questions. Freddie Pike met me at the back of the sanctuary after the morning worship service. He asked to speak to me. Jay went to pick up Jake from the nursery while Freddie delivered some unbelievable news. He said that my seminary admissions process had sparked some conversations among the church staff. "The church wants to help pay for your first semester. I don't know how much you need, but we set aside $1,200." I didn't even have words to answer him. It never crossed my mind that my church would help pay for my first semester. The fact that my home church stepped up and did that just blew me away. To have someone invest in me and believe in me was a gift! Given my life, given the difficulty of the journey from the adoption to the academics to the relationships, it was a grace-gift on every level and completely orchestrated by God. It never crossed my mind that God was (and is) able to make the impossible, possible.

The next day, I decided to look for childcare. I found out there was a day care center near our home that would take children one day a week, so I called them about my need for a Monday spot. The person I spoke to checked their enrollment and told me no spots were available. Next, I called friends and asked if they knew of anyone who would keep a child in their home. No one did. A week passed, and there were no good leads.

Then the phone rang. It was the day care center I had called first. "A child who only attended on Mondays has moved, and there is now one spot available. Would you like to reserve the spot?" I simply said, "Yes." At that moment, I knew I was going to seminary. I was stunned. Stunned in every way. God had stripped away every seminary excuse. There was no time to overthink my decision—I had to register quickly for classes and do "school things" like buy a notebook, or something! My family and friends were very supportive. They offered to help with the supplies I needed.

The journey to seminary started with a bold promise. "Lord, I will do whatever you tell me to do." The Lord put that promise to the test and, through that process, refined my heart. Even when I tried to find a way to break my promise, God proved to be ever faithful.

The downtown campus of Second Baptist Church in Conway, Arkansas. It was in this sanctuary that I learned that the church was paying for my first year of seminary. So thankful for the provision of God!

CHAPTER 17

God in the Window

I woke up early on my first day of seminary classes, sick to my stomach. I didn't want to go. There were tears ... lots of tears. "This 'seminary thing' might not be for me," I thought. I decided I would go to one class and then reevaluate everything.

I felt as if my life was slipping away from me. Seminary had never been in my plan or even on my radar screen. God had clearly called me to go, and He had provided everything I needed. Yet, it felt unsafe. I was unsure of everything: my ability to succeed and God's ability to use me.

I drove across the Arkansas River on my way to Little Rock. The Interstate 430 bridge is long, and the hills surrounding the water are beautiful. The sun hit the water, and the rich, blue sky made me feel a little better. "Help me get through the day," I prayed.

My seminary classes met at the Arkansas Baptist State Convention (ABSC), located then in downtown Little Rock. At 8:40 a.m., I pulled into the parking lot and took a deep breath. The orientation started at 9:00 a.m. I didn't want to be too early or too late. I wanted to be able to walk in, sit down, get the information I needed, and leave.

I entered the building and checked in at the front desk, where I was directed to the second floor. I stepped off the elevator and made my way to the meeting room. Several male students were visiting with each other. There were lots of laughs, handshakes, and good-natured joking. Immediately, I felt out of place. *"Lord, please help me to hold it together,"* I prayed.

I quickly looked for another female. My eyes scanned the room and landed on Carol. I made a beeline to her. We talked for a few minutes, and several of the other students introduced themselves as well. Everyone was friendly, but there was nothing anyone could say that would calm my nerves.

It was 9:00 a.m. and time for the orientation to begin. I was relieved to get into the classroom and find a spot near the back. Lots of information was shared. I took notes and acted as if I had it all together.

On the inside, I was falling apart. *"Lord, why am I here? This is not for me. I can't do this. I'm not ready."* I was beside myself, quite honestly. I knew I wasn't ready for what God was calling me to do. In my heart, I knew God was preparing me for a speaking ministry that would reach a lot of women. I just didn't know how that was going to happen. I looked at myself, my capabilities, and my background. "It just doesn't match." I thought. "It doesn't make sense. I don't know how in the world this will work out." But I knew, deep in my heart, that God was preparing me, that He was calling me, and that He would make it happen. I had a certainty about it, but I had deep fears at the same time.

Finally, they dismissed us for lunch. In the café area, some of the students shared stories about how God was working in their lives. Most of them were already on church staff or involved in some type of active ministry. I wasn't. I was a mom and a housewife. Many of them had undergraduate degrees from Christian universities. Not me. I had a degree in Home Economics from a state school. On that day, if we were playing the game "Which one is not like the other?" I would've been the clear winner! I felt out of place and alone.

Tears began to build up in my eyes. I really wanted to run to my car and drive away, but I was committed to staying for the day. When I feel overwhelmed, one of my coping mechanisms is to find some way to look busy. I noticed there were lots of pictures lining the hallway. So I decided to take a walk and look at them. Most were portraits of people who had served in various roles at the ABSC or paintings of churches in Arkansas.

As I wandered down the hall toward the orientation classroom, I saw a picture that was different. I walked over for a closer look and recognized War Memorial Stadium. I had been there several times.

As I looked at the picture on the wall, I realized it was a picture that was taken during the Billy Graham crusade that I attended at War Memorial in 1989. The Arkansas Baptist State Convention had partnered with the Billy Graham crusade to bring Billy Graham to Little Rock. Thirteen years later, as I stood in the hallway of the ABSC, my mind went back to that day when my mom, cousin, and I drove from my aunt's house in Benton to the stadium. I thought about that day and how Sandi Patty sang and how Billy Graham preached and how happy I had been to be there experiencing it all.

I studied the picture that was taken with a wide-angle lens from the top of the stadium. It was a bird's eye view of the event, showing the fifty thousand people in attendance, nearly filling the stadium. Reverend Graham was preaching from the center of the field.

Almost immediately, something caught my attention. I saw a girl and her mother just three rows in front of the person who took the picture. Nervous excitement welled up inside of me.

I caught my breath as I peered closer and could clearly see that it was my mom and me. The hair bows in my hair gave it away; my mom had made them for me. The back of my mom's head was so familiar and so reassuring to me. Tears started to flow. I was so overwhelmed by the picture and what it meant to me at that vulnerable moment.

As I looked at the picture in disbelief, the Lord held me there and said some amazing things to my heart.

First, the Lord reminded me about the pain that I associated with my "nursery window" experience. *"I've been in the window of your life every second of every day. You have never been alone."* I could visualize God peering down from heaven. Seeing me, cheering for me, and welcoming me to His world. In that moment, I had no doubt that God was in the window of my life.

Second, the Lord reminded me that He had a plan for my life and would use everything—the hard times and the good times—to accomplish His plan. *"Lie down,"* He added. I knew God was confronting my need to be in control.

The Holy Spirit brought to my mind the story of Abraham. God called Abraham to lay his son Isaac on the altar and to sacrifice him as a form of worship. That moment must have been the hardest moment in Abraham's life. Isaac was the son that God had promised to provide, who would lead to the development of God's chosen people, the Israelites. The call of God to lay Isaac on the altar and to sacrifice him made no sense at all. In fact, it seemed to go against everything that was right. But in that nail-biting moment, Abraham laid Isaac on the altar and trusted God to provide.

I've heard the story of Abraham and Isaac more times than I can count. But, looking at that picture on my first day of seminary, the story took on a new meaning. I knew I had to lay my life on the altar. I knew I had to give up control and obey God's call. I had to trust God to provide and to keep His promises to me even if the path didn't make sense. The call to teach women the Bible was the call on my life. God was going to accomplish that plan, but I had to "lay down" my plan and begin to trust His.

Third, God told me that seminary was just the beginning. Honestly, I wanted seminary to be the last hard thing God called me to do. But the call of God was going to continue to move me outside of my comfort zone. I needed to get comfortable with the idea of being uncomfortable. God used the picture to remind me that He had a plan for my life, and He was going to accomplish His plan in and through me.

My years in the desert had taken a toll on me. I was struggling to believe God would use someone like me, someone who had run from Him and His plan. Questions like, "Why would God ever want to use me?" and "What can I do that will really make a difference?"

played out in my mind. Little did I know that God was going to teach me that my role in His plan was simple. I was to be obedient and surrender to Him. That was it. I didn't have to come up with the plan or even have the ability to make the plan happen. My job was to be available and willing.

I think there are people who rush into God's plan, and they want it and thrive in it. And then there are other people, like me, who struggle with it. I've struggled with His plan all along. Everything ties in with how my life began, with my adoption, to walking through different hard things in my life. There was this fear of just letting go. If I let go, what did that mean? Where would I end up? What would I be expected to do?

On that very first day of seminary, I was taking a huge, terrifying step of faith. Just being there was hard for me because I didn't think I belonged. When I walked over and saw that picture hanging on the wall, it was shocking and at the same time, it wasn't. It was one more way God was calling me to let go of control and trust Him.

During that first seminary lunch break, God wrecked my life. He crashed the walls of limiting Him and calling the shots. When I was thirteen years old and attending the Billy Graham crusade, I had no idea that God was capturing that moment in time. It had been a great experience, but it wasn't a milestone in my life. I didn't think about it every day or even every year. I love that, because the takeaway for me is that we are just on this journey, just living life. We all have experiences. We all have struggles, valleys, and mountains, and we are so in the middle of everything that we don't know what's significant. But God does. He is orchestrating our lives to help us know who He is and how He works.

For me, the nursery window began at my adoption. I associated that window with feelings of being isolated and alone. Those feelings impacted my life and my relationship with God and others. For many years, I missed the life that *is* because I was hanging on to the life that *never was*. I was chasing a life that was never mine to live; a life that I charted, a life that I controlled, a life that made sense to me. And even though I knew down deep that I didn't want that life, it was hard for me to accept that I didn't have the chance to live it.

God's plan for me began with adoption, but that was only the beginning. God placed me in the right place, at the right time, with the right people, and He was going to fulfill His right plan! And every single moment of the way, He was right there, not only in the nursery window, but also in the window of my life. *He is God in the Window!*

Billy Graham Crusade in Little Rock, Arkansas in September of 1989. Mom and I are on the second row. I have bows in my hair. This picture reminds me of God's character, love, and grace.

CHAPTER 18

The Card in my Hand

After seeing the Billy Graham picture on the wall of the ABSC, I knew God had a plan for me. I had to complete my first semester of seminary and reevaluate, though. There were so many unknowns. How would we continue to pay for seminary? We didn't expect our church to pay for additional semesters, and we didn't have any savings for school. How would Jake do in day care? He wasn't crazy about going to his "school" one day a week. Would I be able to pass master-level courses with my background of dyslexia? There was lots of reading in my degree plan. I did my best to keep up, but the academic pace was intense. I look back on pictures from this portion of our life, and it's obvious that I really let myself go. There were no highlights in my hair, and my typical outfit was sweatpants and a T-shirt. We were simply surviving.

I received lots of notes, cards, and well wishes during my first semester of school. One note, from my friend Emily, was a lifeline to me!

"Where God Guides, He Always Provides" was the simple statement written on the card. I am sure I had heard the saying before, but it took on new meaning. I was at a place in my life where I needed God to show me the way. I was desperate for Him to provide all the things I couldn't. I claimed the truth written on the card and read it every day.

One of the very first gifts I received when I started seminary was a set of Bible commentaries from Emily's parents, Jim and Donna Seal. I had never met them, but Emily had told them about me. Initially, I was intimidated by Donna because she was a Christian therapist. I tried to keep my interactions with her brief. I didn't want her to figure out that I didn't have everything together. I look back on that attempt and laugh. Over time, Donna became a dear friend and my mentor; just one more way God provided for me in the years ahead.

My first semester of seminary went well. It was like a revival for my soul. I loved the classes and made some good friends. I was constantly trying to figure out what God was calling me to do and how I was supposed to do it. I knew God had called me to teach women the Bible. By that point, I was sure of it. I had spent lots of time thinking about God's work in my life, and every encounter with the Lord pointed to a teaching ministry for women.

As I thought about the call to teach, I thought about what that call might look like in my life. I knew I might have to travel, and my days might be filled with writing. I didn't know if I would be successful, but I knew I had to try.

I had one big problem that I didn't know how to fix. I hadn't told Jay about my call to ministry from my high school days. I hadn't told him about my call to teach women the Bible. I had no idea how to break the news to him. It seemed wrong for me to say, "Hey, Honey, sorry I forgot to mention this to you, but God called me to teach women, and it may involve incredible sacrifice for all of us."

I simply didn't have a peace about delivering that news to him. I wanted Jay to lead our family. I wanted him to chart the direction for our lives. I knew there was only one thing I could do. I had to pray. I knew I needed to put that in God's hands instead of trying to manipulate or fix the issue myself. Remembering the times from my childhood when I had stormed the gates of heaven on behalf of my abused friend, I prayed boldly and asked the Lord to tell Jay about my calling.

One night, several months into my first year of seminary, Jay made plans for us to go to dinner in Little Rock. We were on a tight budget, so I was excited about going out on a date to a real restaurant. As soon as we sat down, Jay said, "I need to talk to you." I was immediately nervous and wondered what was wrong.

Jay looked at me and said, "I don't know what you are going to think about this, but I am sure of it. I want you to listen to me very carefully." I held my breath. "Andrea, you are going to teach women the Bible. You will travel, and you will speak to women. I don't know what it looks like, but we have to get ready." Jay was serious and determined as he talked. He wanted us to begin to develop a ministry plan right there in the restaurant. We started to dream and brainstorm together, and my heart felt as if it would burst from excitement.

My husband is a rock. He doesn't just dream up ideas for the sake of dreaming. If he says something, it's as good as gold, because he means it. Once Jay was on board with the idea of a teaching ministry, a clear direction was set.

As I sat in the restaurant watching my husband take notes, I was amazed by the goodness of God. My husband was leading our family. He was telling me that I was going to teach women the Bible. "Where God guides, He always provides" was becoming more than a saying; it was becoming a reality in my life. "Thank you, Jesus," I thought, and all I could do was repeat it for the next few weeks, months, and years as we figured out a plan together.

There were so many examples of God's incredible provision during the early years of seminary. God provided financially, although it was hard to make ends meet. Jake managed to survive day care, although he never really liked it. I worked hard, and God gave me an ability to learn. He constantly provided on every level, and I was constantly amazed. And I walked past the picture from the Billy Graham crusade every Monday morning during all three years of seminary. Every time, God spoke truth into my life. "I am here. I've always been here. You have never been alone. You can trust Me. Let go of control and simply follow Me."

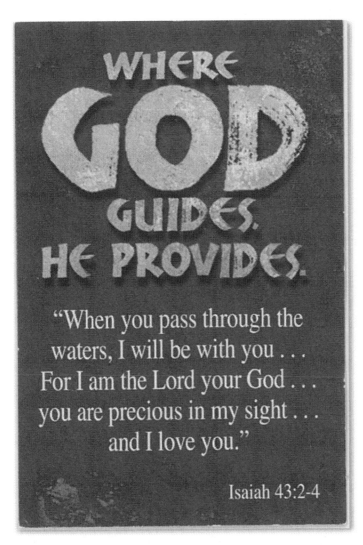

WHERE **GOD** GUIDES. HE PROVIDES.

"When you pass through the waters, I will be with you . . . For I am the Lord your God . . . you are precious in my sight . . . and I love you."

Isaiah 43:2-4

This is the card that my sweet friend Emily gave to me the week before I started Seminary. Without a doubt, God is faithful to provide on every level.

CHAPTER 19

True Vine Ministry

I was in seminary and working on a Master of Arts in Christian Education. God had reaffirmed my call to teach women, time and time again. And my husband was WAY on board with the plan. So it was time to get serious about things.

I already had a name for the ministry. Before I went to seminary, God had spoken to me through His Word and had given a name to me. At the time, I wasn't sure if I would need it, so I tucked the name away and didn't tell anyone about it. Once I realized I was going to have some type of ministry to women, I started to think about the name and realized how perfect it was for my life and my ministry.

In John 15, Jesus said, "I am the true vine, and my Father is the gardener. He cuts off every branch in me that bears no fruit, while every branch that does bear fruit he prunes so that it will be even more fruitful." Verse five goes on to say: "I am the vine; you are the branches. If you remain in me and I in you, you will bear much fruit; apart from me you can do nothing."

There it was, practically in bright lights. A marquee in Vegas couldn't have been clearer. The name of the ministry should be "True Vine Ministry." It was the perfect name! *Jesus is the True Vine, and it's impossible for us to do anything apart from Him.* (I was going to teach women the Bible. I was going to read and write, which had always been "impossible" for me.) *God is the Gardener, and He faithfully prunes us. He cuts away the things that don't belong in our lives, and He uses the hard times to promote growth in and through our lives.* (The prayer I prayed as an eight-year-old girl, "Lord, prune me," was being answered. God was cutting away my need to be in control, and He was teaching me how to trust Him.)

I had a name for the ministry, but that is all I had. God took me through the process of developing the ministry slowly. For the longest time, I only had a name for it and the plans Jay and I brainstormed on our date night. To be honest, that was enough because I was terrified of a public ministry and had no idea how it would take shape or when it would happen.

The lesson God had taught me in my granddad's garden so many years before was helping to shape my life. I needed to follow Jesus. I should never get ahead of Him, I should never get too far behind Him, and I should never try to overshadow Him.

Over the years, I have wondered why I needed to learn the importance of following God at such a young age. Why did God make it so clear to me? I think it was because of my constant need to be in control. Probably more than anything, that has been my journey with God. I have to make the choice daily to trust Him and simply let go of control. I wanted to have power over my life. I felt comfortable when I was calling the shots, determining the direction, and managing my level of investment in a relationship or experience. I never wanted to over-invest. To me, that is how I would get hurt. I kept God and others at a safe, comfortable distance, all the while longing for so much more. I longed to let go and follow God. I longed to love with abandon. I longed to be at peace and take the next step God was calling me to take. But fear and control stood in the way. They were ever present, always impeding the process of following God. Always whispering lies to me.

During this time, God used a sweet lady named Sue in my life. Sue was the women's ministry leader at Second Baptist, and we served together on several committees. One night following a meeting, Sue asked to speak with me. I will never forget the determined look on her face as she said, "Andrea, God has a big plan for your life. It's bigger than the work you're doing at the church. I just feel like you need to get ready." Sue had no idea how God was using her in that moment to reassure me that God was, in fact, preparing me for a public ministry called True Vine. I thanked Sue and tucked her words away in my heart.

CHAPTER 20

Life with Jake

I have always wanted to be a mom. Growing up, I babysat every weekend and volunteered in the church nursery. I loved kids, and I loved the idea of having kids. When Jake was born, it was a dream come true for me.

Even though I was in seminary, I was very focused on Jake and raising him to love Jesus. I had the idea that if I followed a step-by-step parenting plan, Jake would be on board and follow it. That idea quickly changed! Jake was high energy and never accepted the rules at face value. He kept us on our toes from day one. He was a lot of fun even though we had challenging moments.

Parenting Jake opened a whole new world to me because I had always found safety in rules. I wanted to look "good" or achieve a certain end, and I saw the rules as the path to get there. Because of the way God made him, Jake looked at a situation and questioned, "Is there a better way? Why do we have to do it like that?"

There was a natural tension early on in our relationship. I just wanted Jake to follow the rules, and he naturally wanted to question them. God was really shaping both of us through the parent/child relationship. The reality is that rules are good and should be followed, but you don't have to follow them blindly; you can question them, look at them, and think of different ways to do things. Jake has taught me to look at things critically and to not accept the status quo. He has shown me how to be OK with trying things and failing and pushing myself outside my comfort zone.

Because the "rules for the sake of having rules" strategy was not going to work, we learned a different strategy for parenting Jake. We learned to give him options. Before, I would tell him, "Tomorrow you are wearing the red shirt." And Jake would automatically say, "I'm not wearing the red shirt!" And I would respond, "Yes, you are!"

Instead, I learned to say, "I have put three shirts on the bed, and you get to choose whichever shirt you want to wear!" We gave Jake ownership in the process, and he thrived in that environment. That's a simple example of how our lives changed in regard to parenting Jake.

My nice and neat parenting plans were no match for Jake Lennon. He was large and in charge from the moment he arrived. We started giving him options, and we started giving him ownership. He settled in and thrived because of that. When I first became a mom and held Jake in my arms, he was my project. I was going to shape him and mold him into this perfect person who loved God and served others. That was the plan. Thankfully, God sent a child who would push me, try me, and be used by God to mold *me*!

One night, Jake was lying in bed. He was six years old at the time. We were saying our nighttime prayers, and Jake looked at me and said, "I want to go to Heaven when I die. I want to be with you, and I want to be with Jesus in Heaven." We sat down as a family, and Jay and I both talked with him about what it meant to be a Christian. And he knew it. "Jesus died for me, I want Jesus in my heart, and I want to follow Jesus." Jake bowed his head and asked Jesus to save him. There was a significant change in Jake, even as a young child, after his salvation. He was baptized at Second Baptist, and we all laughed as we watched his video testimony prior to his baptism. "I want to be 'bapt-it-zed' to show others that I love Jesus."

As Jake grew, I learned so much from parenting him. Once, when Jake was young, he was sick with a stomach bug. He was throwing up a lot, and he had never had anything like that. He didn't know what to do, and since Jay and I were first-time parents, we weren't sure what to do either.

Jay and I were both kneeling next to Jake's bed just trying to comfort him, and I told him, "Just close your eyes and go to sleep." He looked at me and said, "If I close my eyes, I can't see you." "It's OK," I said. "I'm not going to leave you. Even if you can't see me, I'm still here." The moment I said it, the Lord reminded me that the same is true of our relationship with Him. That taught me about the Lord and my own journey with God; even when we can't see Him or feel Him or sense Him, He's very much there. I would never have left Jake when he was sick, and God will never leave us.

Parenting Jake has been very good for me, both then and now. We have a strong relationship, and we know how to read each other. Jake has always been a leader, and he has always thought outside the box. Life with Jake is an adventure! I am his biggest fan and thank God for him every single day.

All ready for Thanksgiving!

Jake taking a break in Disney.

This picture is a family favorite! Jake and Jay having fun at Disney World.

Success for Jake in South Arkansas!

CHAPTER 21

Pink Carpet and Flowered Wallpaper

Jay, Jake, and I started house-hunting during my second year of seminary. Interest rates were good, and the house where we were living was beginning to feel cramped with our growing family. Our budget was tight, though, and I was a little nervous about taking too big of a financial risk. It was important to me, and to us as a family, to make sure we kept our house payment low so I could continue down the path of ministry.

We looked at houses all over Conway and eventually found a wonderful subdivision called Mallard Crossing. It was full of older homes, but they still looked updated and nice. We drove around and initially found a house we liked and made an offer on it. The offer fell through. One day we were driving around again and saw a house with a "For Sale By Owner" sign. When we drove by the house and looked at it for the first time, I thought, "This is the type of house I've dreamed about!" We called the owners and asked if we could see it. They showed us the house, and we fell in love with it. It had a beautiful front lawn and backyard. We really could see our family living there. The split-floor plan with three bedrooms and two bathrooms would work perfectly for our family.

The yard had big, beautiful trees that I knew we could hang a tire swing from. The kitchen was twice the size of the one I had, so that was a big plus.

Once we were inside the house, however, there were some issues. The carpeting we walked on was brand new but Pepto-Bismol pink. The big, mauve flowers on the wallpaper made me wince. The ceilings were covered in popcorn finish. The linoleum in the kitchen was dated and in bad condition. All of the fixtures were old-fashioned brass, and the fireplace needed to be renovated. The list of things I wanted to update was long and expensive.

Jay and I had a serious talk after we finished looking at the house. We agreed it was structurally sound and had the right floor plan, but the cosmetic issues were significant. We decided we would find a way to take care of the updates and could definitely make the house work for us.

We made an offer, and this one was accepted! We moved into the house, and I started ripping that wallpaper off the wall on the first day. Some of the wallpaper came off easily, and other parts didn't want to come off at all. (I know I removed a layer or two of drywall in more than one spot!)

My can-do personality kicked into high gear. I was determined to update everything and all in the first year. The only problem was that we didn't have one extra dollar. Not one. We were constantly praying for milk and diaper money, and we barely made it from paycheck to paycheck. God was gracious to us, and we didn't miss a meal, but we ate lots of eggs.

For years, the house stayed the same as it was on the day we bought it. The kitchen walls were bare until we finally saved up enough money to paint them. We would slowly do one project and then realize ten more projects needed to happen.

I read "miserly mom" books and tried to meet as many needs as possible without using financial resources. During one conversation with a group of friends who were talking about ways to cut back on their expenses, my ears perked up. I thought I might discover some new ideas. The ideas the girls shared were far from the reality we faced. One said, "I'm going to cut out my magazine subscriptions." Another said, "We are only going to eat out once a week." I stayed silent. "And here I am, watering down my son's milk," I thought. When our finances were tight, life was stressful.

What was difficult for me to understand was the fact that Jay and I had always lived within our means. We had worked hard to be responsible with our finances. We tithed faithfully and with grateful hearts. We were being obedient to God's plan for our lives by surrendering to ministry, yet, we had to stretch a quarter and make it have the impact of a dollar. I cut every possible corner. We lived on the bare necessities, and there were no extras.

Our Friday night routine consisted of taking Jake to Walmart and letting him play with the toys. On the way out, we would stop at the Sam's Choice soft drink machine and each get a 25-cent drink.

There were days when I cried over our finances. I looked at other people around us and wondered why our life couldn't be like theirs. To me, it seemed like everyone was getting a promotion, bonus, new job, great perks, or some kind of financial blessing that constantly eluded us. This situation went on for years.

"Where was God's blessing?" I desperately wanted to ask. But I never asked it aloud because it didn't seem

spiritual, and I wanted to be spiritual. Part of me believed I didn't deserve the blessing and favor of God. The other part of me believed I had to earn it by doing acts of obedience. I was confused about so many things. Still, I continued to go to seminary and made plans for the future, hoping that one day our finances would improve.

CHAPTER 22

Andrew

While at the doctor for a routine visit, I updated my paperwork in the waiting room. Pregnant women were sitting all around me. Worn out from balancing our checkbook, my classes, and life as a wife and mom to a toddler, all I could think was, "I'm so glad I'm not pregnant!" Halfway through seminary, I felt like I was halfway to figuring out what God had for us next. When the nurse called my name, I followed her to the back for the usual weight and blood pressure check. (One of my all-time least favorite moments in life!)

Then the doctor came in, and we visited for a few minutes. As we talked he said, "I think we should do a pregnancy test." I laughed out loud. Then I explained that I was tired because of the pace of my life. The doctor insisted I take the test anyway. I finally agreed.

I peed in a cup. I went back to the exam room and waited. Around ten minutes passed. Then I heard the nurse say, "Dr. Cole, it's positive." With so many women at the office that day, I thought, "They can't be talking about me!"

As soon as Dr. Cole walked into the room, I knew they had been talking about me. The smile on his face said it all. I laid down on the examination table, put my hands over my head, and said, "I'm not ready for this." I was stunned as Dr. Cole put the ultrasound machine on my belly, and we heard a strong heartbeat.

While our first pregnancy was planned and even over-planned, this one was not. I was in seminary and I thought, "God clearly has this call on my life for ministry, and I want to fully embrace it." Looking back, I think I was really trying to get my significance from my call to ministry. And even though I never would have admitted it, I probably thought, "Ministry is how I'm going to make my mark on this world. It's how I'm going to make my life count." As a result, I wasn't sure if it was the right time to have another child.

Since it had taken so much effort to get pregnant with Jake, we had thought another pregnancy wouldn't happen if we weren't putting a lot of work into it. So we decided to just leave it up to the Lord. We weren't going to try, but we weren't going to not try either. I got pregnant the first month.

The pregnancy itself was easier in that I only threw up once a day for the forty weeks. I continued with my seminary classes, and while we were on Christmas break, Andrew made his grand appearance. The timing really was perfect!

The day Andrew was born, I woke up with contractions. I knew what they were this time and told Jay we needed to go to the hospital because they were coming pretty regularly.

We took Jake to a friend's house, and my mom started to make her way to Conway from Harrison. We went by the preschool and paid Jake's registration for the following year and drove to the hospital. By that time, the contractions had stopped. They checked me, and I was dilated to a four, so they said, "We're going to go ahead and keep you." They started a drip of Pitocin, and I had the baby within a few hours. Andrew was born on December 11, 2003. He weighed 6 pounds and 15 ounces, just like Jake.

Andrew was just beautiful. When he came out, and they laid him on me, I can't describe the intense love that I felt for him when I looked into his eyes. It was like in one second God in His goodness and grace wiped away all of the fear and worry that was in my heart. I was so locked in on that baby, loving that baby, and caring for him. We never looked back.

As when Jake was born, it was important to me to look at Andrew through the nursery window before we left the hospital. The hospital staff kept trying to discharge us, and I kept telling them that I needed them to take Andrew back to the nursery. They did and with tears in my eyes, I looked through the window and said, "I see you! You are mine! I will love you forever!"

I took a couple of weeks off after Andrew was born and then hit the ground running. We continued on in ministry; we continued on in serving. In fact, the very first time we took Andrew to church, he was three weeks old, and he sat in his baby carrier as I worked the women's ministry table in the lobby of the church.

I had a connection with Andrew from the first moment I saw him. I would spend hours just holding him. I couldn't soak up enough of him and his personality. He was so laid-back. Andrew was his happiest whenever Jay or I held him. We totally spoiled him and just held him for hours and hours. There was something so healing about that for me because the pace of my life had always been running at 100 miles per hour. I thrived on having more than one project going on at a time. This was the first time I realized it was important for me to learn how to be still. With Andrew, we didn't care about the schedule or all the rules. If he wanted to eat, I was going to feed him! It was like a 100 percent change from how we had interacted with Jake just three years earlier.

Jake was a great big brother. He liked to hold Andrew and talk to him. He would try to toss a ball to him and play big-boy games like cars and trucks. While their personalities were different, they had a connection that was real from the beginning. Andrew rarely cried, and he slept a lot. He sucked his middle two fingers and was so easygoing.

One day I was shopping in Walmart with Andrew when a total stranger came up to me and introduced himself as a doctor. He said that the shape of Andrew's head had caught his eye and suggested taking Andrew to see our pediatrician. I immediately made an appointment, and our pediatrician confirmed the news that there was something wrong.

Andrew needed to be seen at Arkansas Children's Hospital. In addition, we needed to begin physical therapy for his neck. Andrew was diagnosed with torticollis, which is similar to a crick in your neck. For a baby, this is a problem because they don't know how to work the crick out of their neck. And even though we changed his sleeping position regularly, we never noticed that he always laid on the same side of his head. The doctors decided that Andrew needed to be fitted for a helmet and go through several months of physical therapy.

We made it through the helmet process, which was stressful and required flexibility. We never knew what the day held. At any given time, we had to drop everything and go to Children's Hospital to get the helmet adjusted. The added financial pressure paled in comparison to our worries about Andrew. There wasn't a mountain that we wouldn't have moved for either of our boys.

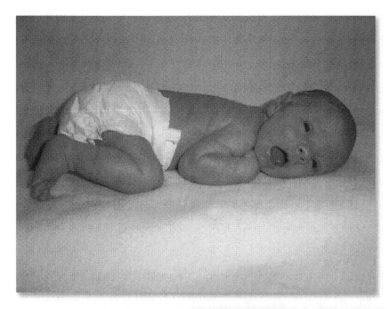

Andrew loved being held. He was an easy baby.

Andrew swinging in the backyard on the playground built by Jay and Granddad Morris.

Andrew at Magic Springs in Hot Springs, Arkansas.

Jake and Andrew at a pumpkin patch in Green-brier, Arkansas. Jake was a great big brother and Andrew loved to watch Jake.

CHAPTER 23

Let My People Go!

Seminary was challenging and not just because of the material. Each summer, and during January, I traveled to Fort Worth to complete I-term classes that were offered on-campus. An I-term class was intense. It required the student to do all their reading prior to arriving on campus. The class was given in a one-week period. The student would sit in class from 8:00 in the morning until 5:00 in the evening, Monday through Friday. The mid-term was given on Wednesday afternoon, and the final was given on Friday. Then the student had two weeks to finish a research paper.

This was brutal for anyone on a normal seminary schedule, but sometimes I would take two I-terms back to back. I would go for a week, take one I-term, and then either come home for a day or stay in Fort Worth. During those days, I reminded myself of the card my friend had given me: "Where God guides, He always provides."

All of the time when I was in school, I either had Jake as a toddler, or a nursing baby (Andrew) plus a toddler. I couldn't just travel and study by myself; I often had to take them with me. My entire family was involved in the process. My sister kept Jake during the early years. Jay, Jake, and Andrew would go to campus with me during the later years. Sometimes my parents would go and help with the kids. Nothing about the process was easy.

At one point, I knew I needed to be on campus in Texas for a week. So Jay, Jake, Andrew, and I made the six-hour drive from Conway to Fort Worth and settled in a small hotel room on the SWBTS campus. I should have known the week was going to be challenging when we hadn't made it thirty minutes from home before Jake threw up in the car, and Andrew's diaper exploded with diarrhea.

My class schedule that week was brutal. I was in class from 7:45 a.m. until lunch. Then I would run back to the room, eat a quick lunch, and nurse Andrew. I had to stick closely to my nursing schedule because being in a room full of guys, I didn't want it to be obvious that I was lactating! I would hurry back to class and finish by 5:00 p.m.

Jay had been stuck in a small hotel room with the kids trying to work and keep them quiet. I would try to take over at the 5:00 p.m. mark and be the fun mom. Our family would go out to dinner at Chuck E. Cheese or some place with a playground. We would get the kids in bed and asleep by 9:30 p.m. I would then go into the bathroom to study my notes so Jay could sleep. I would usually study until 2:00 a.m. and sleep from 2:00 a.m. until 6:00 a.m. I would wake up, feed the boys, and try to get them ready for the day.

One night I was sitting on the bathroom floor when I got tickled at the state of my life. It was one of those moments in life when you either laugh or cry. There I was, in a small hotel bathroom in Texas, studying Baptist history. I started to laugh and couldn't stop. So much for being in control!

The lowest moment in my seminary journey came when I realized my degree plan actually required half of my hours to be completed on campus in Fort Worth. I had been under the impression that only a third had to be completed on campus. While I had taken the right classes, I had taken too many of them at the extension campus in Little Rock. The only solution was to spend an extra summer in Fort Worth taking classes that were not in my degree plan. Andrew was nursing, so that meant that he and one other person had to go with me. It was a lot of extra money, time, and effort.

I don't think I had ever been able to fully relate to Moses and his intense desire to get the Israelites out of

Egypt and to the Promised Land until my last semester of seminary. (Granted SWBTS wasn't Egypt, and I wasn't Moses, and the fine folks that I interacted with weren't Pharaoh, but hopefully you get my point!) Like Moses, I found myself saying, "Let my people go!" I desperately wanted to finish seminary and get on with life. I wanted to focus more attention on my family and my calling.

After many tears and adding up the expenses (in time and money) for one more summer in Fort Worth, I decided I didn't have it in me. I was going to quit school. This was a hard decision for me because I'm not a quitter. To be fair, I can be a whiner and a complainer but definitely not a quitter.

At a low point, I called my parents to tell them the news. Thankfully, they wouldn't have it! My dad helped me to see that I was so close and while it was unfortunate I had to take extra hours, "we" could do it. Mom packed her bag, and she and I and Andrew headed to Fort Worth. By God's grace, I completed my last I-term and acquired enough on-campus hours to graduate.

SWBTS was gracious and also allowed me to count an internship that I did at my home church in Conway as on-campus hours, too. That was a HUGE blessing because I could be at home with my guys. So, after hours of studying, reading, writing, praying, and crying, I graduated from seminary with a Master of Arts in Christian Education. It had been seventy six hours of master-level classes, and I was exhausted.

Since school was so difficult for me as a child, I couldn't do anything but give all the glory to God when I graduated from seminary with a master's degree and a 4.0 grade point average. God is so good!

I am so thankful for my time at Southwestern Baptist Theological Seminary. I was exposed to incredible theological material. I often tell people, "When I went to seminary, I thought I would learn so much." And I did. But what I really learned was how much I didn't know. That was an important step for me because it taught me how to be a lifelong learner. I was exposed to information I had never known. I was challenged to think about it and wrestle with it and began to nail down my beliefs. Because of my time at SWBTS, I truly believe education is vital in our faith journey. I had wonderful professors, and I have wonderful contacts as a result of my time there. I'm so thankful God led me to SWBTS. The extension campus in Little Rock and the relationships I built during my time there have been invaluable to me—truly a picture of God's amazing love and grace.

When I started seminary, Jake had just turned one. When I graduated from seminary, it was the weekend of Andrew's first birthday. Looking back, I'm so glad I completed my degree while the kids were little since they don't remember those exhausting, stressful years. On the other hand, Jay and I (and our family) will never forget them!

Graduating from Southwestern Baptist
Theological Seminary in December of 2004.
I was thankful to complete my degree,
and begin serving the Lord in ministry. It
was a LONG ROAD to this point in my life.
God's grace is always sufficient.

CHAPTER 24

Leading, Loving, and Serving Others

During my last semester of seminary, I did an internship at my home church of Second Baptist in Conway. After graduating, I transitioned to volunteering there. Mark Dance was my pastor, and we had talked about the possibility of me joining the staff as an assistant co-ordinator in the area of education. For both of us, it wasn't a matter of "if" but "when." In my volunteer position, I helped lead and organize Bible studies, small groups, and discipleship. I loved it all!

One day, out of the blue, my phone rang. My boys were running around the house and yelling. I hurried to the bathroom and shut the door in order to try to block some of the noise.

My friend, Robby Tingle, was on the phone. He had an amazing opportunity to drop in my lap. It turned out that his boss and mentor, Jimmie Sheffield, was looking for a minister of education to serve on a part-time and interim basis at Second Baptist Church in Jacksonville, Arkansas. In the Arkansas Baptist world, Jimmie was (and is) a big deal. Robby wholeheartedly recommended me for the position and wanted to know what I thought.

"No way. I can't do that!" was my first reaction. My plan was to serve on staff at my home church in a coordinator role. My home church was comfortable and safe. I knew the people, and the people knew me. Working at another church where I was the minister of education, not an assistant, terrified me. "Would the people there accept me? Would they listen to me? Would they follow me? Would I even know what to do?" These were just a few of the questions that ran through my mind. Just the thought of having an interview with Jimmie Sheffield was overwhelming to me.

Looking back, I can see a pattern in my life. When given an opportunity to step out and try something new or something "big," I always try to talk others out of asking me to do it. Always. Being recommend or referred for a position or a role makes my stomach sink, and I immediately come up with arguments such as, "I can't do that! I'm not ready!" I can also get very "helpful" during these times and suggest others who I think would thrive in the role. Probably one of the most consistent works that God has done in my life is to put me in places where this happens. Then He challenges me to step out in faith anyway. He challenges me to push past the fear and the doubt and to trust Him to do a work in me and through me.

Even with my hesitation, Robby encouraged me to talk to Jimmie about the position in Jacksonville. He encouraged me to be open to the possibility. I was intimidated at the idea of an interview, let alone the job itself. However, Jay and I had been praying about the next step for me after seminary. This job would provide needed income and great experience, too. I agreed to the interview, but that was as far as I would go.

I drove to Jacksonville and felt sick the entire drive. My mind was going in a hundred directions, trying to anticipate questions and come up with good answers.

I walked into the church, found the office, and took a seat. Jimmie walked out of his office and introduced himself to me. I knew who he was. He had been a guest lecturer in one of my seminary classes, and I had seen him at the Arkansas Baptist building many times. I had never talked to him, of course.

The interview was surprisingly easy. Jimmie asked about my family, calling, testimony, and vision for educational work in the church. Somehow, I made it through the interview and was surprised when Jimmie offered the position to me. A year later, Jimmie told me I had the job before I arrived at the church. He had done his homework and had been told by several people that I was ready for the position.

I was nervous and excited about this new opportunity. Second Jacksonville needed some strong leadership in the area of education. They needed a fresh vision, and they were willing to make changes and try new ideas. I wasn't sure what was ahead, but I knew God would show me what to do.

Working at Second Jacksonville was going to be a big change for our family. The church was a fifty-minute drive from our home, a longer commute than I was used to. I would work two days a week, all day Sunday and all day Tuesday. The rest of the time, I could be at home with the boys.

While I was finding my way with the new job, the people of Second Jacksonville were so good to me. They loved me, allowed me to try new things, and made me feel like I belonged. While I was working there, I met Tammy Fletcher, the women's ministry leader. Tammy and I shared a deep love for God and His Word, and we led several women's Bible studies together. We could often be found sitting at a restaurant, enjoying lunch as we discussed how to pour into the lives of the women who would come.

It was at Second Jacksonville where I learned the importance of trusting God to show me how to lead, love, and serve others. I truly believe my time there was a pivotal point in my ministry life. It was there that I experienced the restoration of God in regard to running from my call to ministry. God showed me it is never too late to obey. When He does a redeeming work in our lives, He goes to the core of who we are and changes us. When He changes us, He changes the direction of our lives. Everything about my life changed when I stepped into my calling and trusted God to show me day by day how to follow Him. I had a new sense of peace and purpose. I learned how to have confidence in God and His willingness to work in me and through me.

With my sweet friend Tammy at Second Baptist Church in Jacksonville, Arkansas.

My very first office! I loved serving the Lord and the wonderful people at Second Baptist Church in Jacksonville, Arkansas.

I served on the women's ministry team at Second Baptist Church in Conway, Arkansas. I learned so much about women's ministry from these sweet ladies.

I have great memories of serving on staff at Second Baptist Church in Jacksonville, Arkansas with Joe Francis and Jimmie Sheffield.

CHAPTER 25

Loving God Inside Out

About a year into my time of serving at Second Baptist in Jacksonville, my sweet friend Sue, the women's ministry leader at my home church in Conway, played a trick on me. She asked, "Andrea, if you were to lead a women's retreat, what would you teach?" (Remember that Sue knew God was preparing me for some type of ministry to women.) I quickly rattled off four or five ideas. One of them was the topic, "Loving God Inside Out." I had already been jotting down some material on that topic, even though I didn't have any retreats booked at the time. Sue looked at me and said, "That sounds great! How about leading our retreat in April?" I was stunned. A nervous excitement hit the pit of my stomach as I told Sue I would be honored to lead the retreat.

The retreat was held at a conference center about forty-five minutes from Conway. During the drive there, I was praying with passion: "Lord, you have to come back right now!" I prayed for the rapture all the way because I was so terrified to lead. Jesus didn't come back, and I made it to the retreat center. I was amazed when I walked in and saw the room filled with women from my home church. I led four, one-hour sessions and probably talked so fast due to my nerves. Thankfully, I survived the retreat and so did all of my sweet church friends!

After the retreat was over, Sue came to me with a basket full of gifts. She gave me the biggest hug and told me the retreat was a total success. I was so thankful for her sweet words of encouragement! One of the gifts in the basket was a metal wall hanging of the word "Imagine." As Sue handed it to me, she said, "I just want you to imagine all of the possibilities." I knew the Lord was using Sue to encourage me to dream big in that moment. I began to imagine a life that was totally sold out to Jesus. I felt a deep sense of tension in my heart that was so real—a tension that came from the tug of war that was going on inside of me. I wanted to embrace all of the plans God had for me, but I also wanted to play it safe. The memory of that tension is still with me today. Thankfully, so is the wall hanging! It is on display in my dining room, and I walk by it every single day.

I will always thank God that the first retreat I led was for my home church. When God called me to begin True Vine Ministry, I knew my role was to serve women in different local churches. True Vine was never established to take the place of a local church for me or anyone else. Rather, True Vine provides a way for me to serve as many local churches as possible. The local church is so important because it provides accountability, consistent community, and serves as a rally point for believers to reach their homes, communities, nation, and the world with the gospel of Jesus. I love my home church of Second Baptist in Conway and will always be actively involved in the mission of serving through her as well as through True Vine Ministry.

CHAPTER 26

Write It Down

After about fifteen months of serving together, Jimmie's time at Second Baptist in Jacksonville was coming to an end. It was time for the church to hire a permanent pastor. The church leadership made it clear to me that I was welcome to stay in my role as minister of education.

Even though it seemed like an obvious (and financially wise) choice to stay in my job, I felt a growing tug of war in my heart. I loved serving in the local church because it felt safe to me. I was surrounded by people I liked, and we were working together to accomplish God's plan.

Even from childhood, the local church had been a place for me to call home. I knew how to "do church."

The struggle came from knowing clearly that God had called me to teach women His Word. My role on a local church staff would never involve solely teaching the Bible. The role would involve more organization and administration. While that is not a bad role, it was not the true calling on my life.

I knew God was faithful and would show me the way, but I didn't know what steps I should take. Up until that point, I had led some women's Bible studies and the "Loving God Inside Out" retreat for my home church in Conway, but that was it. There was the possibility of other teaching opportunities, but nothing was certain. One morning I woke up and knew I had to tell someone about this growing tug of war going on inside of me. I felt as if I was drowning in my call.

As much as I needed to talk to someone, I felt physically sick at the thought of putting God's clear direction into words. I was tempted to think, "If I don't say it, then I won't have to do it."

I drove to work that morning and decided I would talk to Jimmie about my calling to teach women the Bible. I decided I would tell him everything. I prayed a very bold prayer during my drive: "Lord, write my calling on his heart. Give him a desire to help me."

I walked into the office that morning and asked Jimmie if he had time to talk. I was no longer intimidated by him and knew that he loved me and my family and that all of us would stay in touch, even after Jimmie and I stopped working together. I was also very fond of his sweet wife, Mrs. Annette.

Jimmie agreed to talk to me, and once I started talking, I couldn't stop. I told Jimmie everything. I told him about God calling me to teach women the Bible—the Kay Arthur video moment, the call at the Beth Moore conference to go to seminary, the Billy Graham picture at the ABSC, God telling Jay about my calling, the name of True Vine Ministry, dyslexia, and adoption. I told Jimmie about my fears and anxieties and struggles. I was certain that I couldn't do what God was calling me to do. I was stuck in every way. Stuck between living a life of faith and a life I controlled. I remember saying, "I feel like I'm drowning. I can't breathe."

Jimmie listened to every word. Then he looked at me and said, "Write it down." "What do you mean?" I asked. He replied, "Everything that you told me, write it down. God will show you what to do with it." I later asked Jimmie what he thought about our conversation. I was amazed when he said, "I've heard lots of testimonies over the years, but yours is one of the most powerful ones I've heard." Jimmie told me that following our conversation, he knew God was calling him to help me. He was totally on board with True Vine Ministry. It was many years later when I told Jimmie about my bold prayer, "Lord, write my calling on his heart." I am forever grateful that God did!

I went on a camping trip the following day with my family. I sat by a small river and started to write everything down. I wrote down what God had done, what He was doing, and what I longed for Him to do in the future. As I look back on my life and pinpoint pivotal moments, this was one of them.

I always encourage women to write their story down. It can be a clarifying process that helps us see the specific plan God has for our lives. As I wrote, God spoke a clear word to me. I didn't hear His voice audibly, but the message was crystal clear. As I looked at the hard parts of my story, God simply said, "These wounds heal." What a sweet word from the Lord. He was letting me know the pain in my life wouldn't always be so intense, and by His grace, the pain I had experienced would help others. Even though I didn't realize it, once I started praying and dreaming and planning for the future, there would be no turning back. Of course, there was still some wrestling I had to do to let go of control!

My dear friends Jimmie and Annette Sheffield. These two mean the world to me. I am beyond grateful for their friendship, love and support.

CHAPTER 27

Passing the Point of No Return

Second Baptist Church in Jacksonville called Steve Walter to serve as their new senior pastor. I committed to stay as minister of education until Steve was settled and knew the direction that God was leading for that position.

Still, I wrestled with my calling. I could stay at Jacksonville on a permanent basis. I loved the people, and they loved me. What had started as a six-month commitment at Jacksonville had turned into a two-year process. Another option was to send my resume to other churches in the state, where I could find another ministry position. At the same time, I had this growing sense of unrest that kept me up at night.

Several months passed. Jay and I continued to pray about the future. I was offered more and more opportunities to teach the Bible at women's ministry events around the state of Arkansas. Jimmie and others at the Arkansas Baptist State Convention (ABSC) started sharing my name with churches. The ABSC also invited me to speak at statewide events.

Finally, a decision had to be made. I had to focus on serving in the local church or take a leap of faith and focus on developing True Vine Ministry.

I am a firm believer in the fact that God speaks clearly to His people through His Word. There is nothing anyone can say to convince me otherwise, since I've heard from the Lord that way too many times to count. When I face a difficult decision, I always ask the Lord to show me His answer through His written Word. This keeps me from playing it safe by leaning on my human emotions or logic.

One week, I was wrestling with my decision and badly needed an answer. I asked God to speak to me through my time in the Bible.

I opened up to my daily Bible reading. That day, I was in Acts 6, a chapter that explains the development of the early church and the role of a deacon. The deacons were asked to take on the responsibility of the widows and wait on the tables so the Apostles could focus on the ministry of the Word.

As I read, my heart began to pound. I knew God was showing me a principle—a principle that would free me to let go of a role that was not meant to be mine forever so I could embrace a role God had on His heart for me since before I was born. *God calls people to embrace different roles for different reasons. When we embrace our God-given roles, the Word of the Lord spreads.* (Acts 6:1-7) There it was! I simply needed to understand the role God had for me, and then I needed to follow Him in simple obedience. If I believed the Bible, and I did, the outcome of this type of life would be so exciting. God's Word would spread!

From the very beginning, God had called me to teach. He had prepared me to teach. He had allowed obstacles to come into my life so that when I taught He would receive the glory. Staying in the local church would be like waiting tables for me. I could do it, but it wasn't what God was calling me to do. God couldn't have been clearer. Now, it was time to respond in obedience and faith.

174

I knew when I let go of working at a church in order to start True Vine, it would be a step that would forever change my life. It would be a step that would take me past the point of no return.

I often teach about the concept of sanctification. Sanctification is the idea that we become more and more like Jesus and less and less like the world. While sanctification is a fancy "two-dollar" spiritual word, it is a practical concept for our lives. Sanctification happens when our hearts value the things of Jesus and heaven over the things (or ways) of this world. The outcome of sanctification is that we follow God's plan even when it makes us uncomfortable or doesn't make sense. That's what True Vine represented to me. It aligned me with Jesus and His plan for my life, rather than my own plan.

I had no idea what my calling would look like on a day-in-and-day-out basis. I had no idea how to start a speaking ministry. Nor did I know if I would be able to sustain a ministry, because I had no speaking engagements on my calendar. This was a step of faith on every level, and I was desperate for God to show me the way. Sometimes God works like that. He doesn't give us the plan; He simply shows us the next step much like the lesson I learned in the garden with my granddad: *Never get ahead of Him, never get too far behind Him, and never try to overshadow Him. Simply follow step by step.* I continued to serve at Second Baptist in Jacksonville for a few more months, but the end was in sight.

I certainly had second thoughts during the next few months. Jay and I were giving up a steady paycheck, and we had no idea how to begin a ministry. I didn't know anyone I could call and ask, "How do you start a ministry?" But God was so good to us during that time of transition. One morning when I woke up doubting, all I could do was pray: "Lord, please help us to know that we are doing the right thing." Within thirty minutes of that prayer, my phone rang two times. Two different people called and asked me to speak at their upcoming women's events. I bowed my head and said, "OK."

There would be moments when I would think, "This is crazy! What am I doing?" Then there would be moments when I was so sure, so positive we were doing the right thing, no one could have convinced me otherwise. God was taking me past the point of no return! Finally, after many years of fighting it, I was willing to go.

CHAPTER 28

Stepping Out

My last day at Second Baptist Church in Jacksonville was bittersweet and unforgettable. I visited each and every Sunday school class to say goodbye and soaked up the sermon and music at the morning worship service. After lunch with sweet friends, I went back to the church and spent several hours thinking and praying. I walked around the church and prayed over every classroom. I went into the sanctuary and knelt at the altar and poured out my heart to the Lord. I prayed for the church and everyone's future. I also prayed for myself and for the testimony I was going to share at the evening service.

That evening, as I stepped to the front of the church, I was nervous. But as I started to talk, God gave me boldness and certainty. I knew I was doing the right thing. I shared with the church about my adoption and how God had been in the window of my life, preparing me for this moment in time. I talked about my love for the local church and how the local church had always been a safe place for me. I told them about how God had called me to teach women the Bible when I was sixteen and how I ran from the call. Then I added, *I am going to start a ministry for women called True Vine Ministry.* I said it, finally said it, out loud.

Following the service, the church hosted a reception for me and my family. My sweet friend Tammy put together a beautiful event. Fresh flowers, amazing food, sweet notes, and a long receiving line made the event simply perfect. I was overwhelmed. It was a sweet day, and I will be forever grateful for my time at Second Baptist Church in Jacksonville, Arkansas.

When I woke up the following Monday morning, reality hit me. It was time to begin True Vine Ministry. To say that I was clueless was an understatement. I had several events on the calendar, and God was about to open the floodgates, but every day was a mystery to me.

Looking back, I see the faithfulness of God in every detail. One detail was the fact that my home was in Arkansas. Arkansas is a close-knit state, where the connections between people are strong. News, both good and bad, travels fast.

In the early days, I didn't do any marketing or promotion. Honestly, I was scared each time I booked an event. While I knew that I was doing what God called me to do, I felt sick every single time I stood in front of a group to share. Thankfully, God placed people in my life who would share my name and promote the ministry for me.

I can't say enough about the folks at the Arkansas Baptist State Convention. They did everything in their ability to help me. Dr. Sonny Tucker, who serves as the executive director, is a dear friend and strong supporter of True Vine. I first met Sonny when he was one of my seminary professors. I took his class on evangelism, and it was like a revival each week. I had a solid connection with Sonny from the very beginning. He saw potential in me as a leader that I didn't see in myself.

During the early years of True Vine, I met with Sonny twice a year. These meetings were invaluable to me. Sonny offered great insight and advice, and I found that I could use our conversations as the basis for a yearly ministry plan. In fact, the inspiration for the writing side of True Vine Ministry came from advice Sonny gave me.

God was faithful to lead each step of the way. He connected me to the right people, and before long, a website, headshots, business cards, and banners were provided for True Vine. Often, people look at this portion of my journey and say, "Andrea, it was easy for you. Things just fell into your lap." While I know what people mean, and I'm so grateful to God for the way He provided, nothing about that time was easy. I was beyond my comfort zone and my ability. I daily fought the urge to hide in my laundry room and act like I was too busy to face the reality that God was creating a ministry—despite me.

I spent a lot of time studying the Bible and writing Bible study material. While my dyslexia wasn't as crippling as it had been in school, I was still worried about reading long passages in public. My solution was to teach one verse of Scripture per speaking event. This meant that I would only need to read a few words out loud. I would practice reading the verse and even memorize it so I could deliver the message with clarity. While it was hard work then, some of my favorite teaching sessions and Bible study material came from this season of my life. My teaching sessions on Romans 12:2, Psalm 25:15, Romans 15:13, and Galatians 5:1 are just a few examples.

I scripted out each event. I would type, word-for-word, what I would say. The thought of that today makes me so tired! Do you know how fast I talk? That is a lot of words to type! Each lesson followed the same outline: introduction, bridge, body, application, and conclusion. I tried to hit the different levels of learning and make a strong application to the lives of the women I spoke to.

I had been convinced that the teaching degree I earned from the University of Central Arkansas was a waste of time and money. I never planned to teach in a school setting, so in my mind, it wasn't necessary. While I was running, though, God was using the decisions I made to prepare me for a future I never dreamed possible.

I remember the day I climbed up the ladder to our attic and searched for a box that had my college handouts and textbooks in it. (My mom raised me to never throw away a handout or textbook!) I found the box and started to dig through it. What a gold mine! I found handouts that reminded me about the different levels of learning, all the ways to structure a lesson, and the importance of making real-life application at the end of each lesson. I read every word and took in every ounce of the material in a fresh new way. God had already taught me how to teach. He had prepared me. Now it was time to start doing it. Oh, how I love His redeeming work in our lives! God never wastes our deserts.

When speaking, I had a rule of thumb: I never looked at the check until I was driving away from the event. I didn't have a set fee or a typical fee range. I took whatever amount the church provided. Sometimes it was $50; other times it was as much as $500. I waited until I was driving home to look at the check so I would not be too excited or too disappointed by the amount.

One day I was speaking at a church, and at the end of the event, I was given a check. This check was made out to True Vine Ministry. I wasn't sure what to do about that. All of my previous checks had been made out to Andrea Lennon. I called the bank and asked if they would cash it for me. The teller said I needed to open a business checking account to cash the check. In order to open a business account, I had to get a tax identification number. In order to get the tax ID number, I had to register with the State of Arkansas. So, in 2007, I officially incorporated True Vine Ministry.

I arrived at the bank to open a business checking account and discovered that it required a $500 balance, which was the amount of my check. I laughed as I drove away from the bank. I was an incorporated ministry and had my very own tax ID number and business checking account, but I didn't have enough money to actually cash my own check. I called my parents as I left the bank and told them the funny story. A few days later, a check arrived in the mail from Mom and Dad. They gave me a sweet gift that would cover the necessary bank balance so that I could actually cash checks and have access to the money, if needed. As I look back, that is one of my favorite stories in the development of True Vine Ministry.

In the middle of juggling the paperwork and headaches that come with a startup, God brought a memory to mind. Ironically, I hadn't put together the significance of the prayer that I prayed when I was eight years old, "Lord, prune me," and the name of the ministry that I was incorporating, True Vine Ministry, until I was filling out the paperwork. God was saving that realization for this moment. A moment in time when I needed a big dose of His reassurance.

I looked at the name True Vine Ministry, and I remembered how I decided to name the speaking ministry based on John 15. To me, the name True Vine represented the idea that apart from Jesus, I could do nothing. As I was thinking about the name and the pruning prayer, in that moment, everything made sense. True Vine was a ministry born out of a deep desire to remain with Jesus and to rid my life of anything that took me away from Him. True Vine was more than a name ... it was a picture of my life and an answer to my simple prayer. In order to follow God, I had to begin True Vine. In order for True Vine to succeed, I had to let go of control. In order to let go of control, I had to trust Him to take me to a place I could never get to on my own.

True Vine was officially in business. And I was officially in shock.

CHAPTER 29

Ministry Growing Pains

The ministry grew quickly. The first year, I booked three events. The next year, I booked seven events. The year after that, I booked twenty events. The next year ... I stopped counting.

So much of this season of my life is a blur to me. Isn't that funny about life? I thought I would never forget it. The truth is, we were just trying to make it from one weekend to the next. Jay and the boys were troopers. I would be home during the week and then travel on the weekends. I led conferences, retreats, and special events. Sometimes I spoke for thirty minutes, sometimes for six hours. I let the host church pick the topic and the Scripture, which stretched my studying and learning since I couldn't always do the same thing week after week.

There was one thing that was the same every weekend, and that was my outfit! Let's face it—nice clothes are important in women's ministry. Our budget was tight, so I had to think of a creative way to find a professional outfit. Then I had an idea. I decided that I only needed one nice outfit since I was in a different church each weekend. I went to the store and put all the clothes money I had into the perfect outfit: pants, blazer, heels, necklace, earrings, and bracelets. I looked professional, and I never had to wonder what to wear when speaking. This plan worked beautifully until social media came on the scene, and women started posting pictures of me week after week. I was busted, and I had to revamp my clothing plan.

When I needed a different outfit, my friends let me borrow clothes and jewelry all the time. In fact, my first speaking outfit came from the closet of my good friend April Kinley. My mom and sister helped, too. They chipped in money and took me on shopping trips. We had the best time finding deals.

During the first few years of True Vine, I took every event that was offered to me. God used our financial need and my "Type A" personality to increase my willingness to serve. Jay and I were on the same page about my need to step out and gain needed experience.

Flexibility is important in my line of work. When I walk into a church, I never know what to expect. I think the same is true for the church. Most of the time, they don't know me. We both have to trust that God has brought us together, and that He is going to work in a powerful way.

I love the women who I get to serve. In the many years of serving the Lord through True Vine Ministry, I only have had two bad experiences. I'm so thankful for that. However, I've had dozens of funny stories! Somehow I seem to attract awkward moments, and it doesn't help that once I'm in an awkward moment, I make it worse by over-analyzing, over-explaining, and over-apologizing. I share these experiences with so much love and joy in my heart. We are all family, and it's good to be able to laugh at yourself and with each other!

A few years ago, I was invited to speak at an event, and the theme was "Whispers of God's Love in the Garden of Life." As beautiful as they sound, themes like this make a speaker wonder, "How can I make that theme relevant to a woman's life and keep it Biblical?" There are so many different angles to approach it from, and narrowing a focus down can be difficult. But they had provided a key verse, which was Psalm 46:10: "Be still and know that I am God." From there, I could plan out my messages.

I arrived at the event and parked my car. I walked into the church, found the women's ministry leader, and set up my book table. The ladies arrived, and the event began. I was scheduled to speak for thirty minutes on Friday night and two hours on Saturday morning. The Friday night session served as an introduction for the weekend. I shared some key thoughts from Psalm 46:10. As I concluded my final thoughts, I felt good about how I had woven the theme of the event into the Scripture and made it applicable to the ladies' lives. I sat down and breathed a sigh of relief.

The women's ministry leader came to the stage and said she had been thinking about our theme and how different tools that are used in the garden can represent our tendencies in life. She said she wanted to play a game that would help us get to know each other. "I'm going to call out a tool that is used in the garden; if you feel like that tool represents you, stand up!"

Looking around, she said, "If you are a watering can, please stand up." There was no response. She moved on, "If you are a shovel, please stand up." Again, nothing. In that moment, I decided that whatever she said next, I was standing up. I love women's ministry leaders, and I am not letting one go down on my watch.

With great emphasis, the women's ministry leader said, "If you are a hoe, please stand up." I popped up and looked around. With great gusto, I said, "I'll be the hoe!" And it was at that moment that I realized what had just happened. Immediately my awkward explaining and apologizing began. "Oh, I don't mean it like that. I'm not that kind of girl! I mean, I'm a hoe ... like I will dig out the truths of Scripture." The women's ministry leader enthusiastically joined in and said to the group, "If you want to be a hoe like Andrea, please stand up!" It was at that moment that she also realized what had happened. I sat down in a hurry and thought, "Come quickly, Lord Jesus!"

My own speaking engagements had their ups and downs, too. There were times when I left a church and thought, "Bless their hearts. I bet that was painful for them to listen to!" Other times I would leave saying, "God, that was great! That was all You!" I finally noticed a pattern—I would think the event went well about every third time.

I tried so hard to do my part. Studying hard. Practicing my reading. Avoiding distractions. (Like not watching TV within twenty-four hours of teaching, never reading a magazine that was in my hotel room, and always making sure that Jay prayed over me before I left our house.) The early years were exhausting. Just like when I was younger, I was trying to control the ministry and force God to bless it by doing all the "right" things. In the process, I missed the joy in the journey.

One of the things I struggled with was wondering if I had done a good enough job. "Did I deliver the message with passion? Did it make sense? Were lives changed? Would I be asked to return? Was I funny? Did the outfit I wore look cute?" There were so many questions and so much insecurity. It took years for me to learn that, as a speaker, I was just one piece of a much bigger puzzle. I also learned that I would never really know what God was doing in a moment to touch and change lives, and that was OK.

Growing pains are hard. They bring you to the end of yourself and force you to your knees. Thankfully, God was laying the groundwork for freedom in my life. I didn't know it at the time, but He was bringing me to the end of myself and growing my hunger for a relationship that was about Him instead of about me.

Nothing excites me more than sharing God's Word with others! This picture was taken at Park Hill Baptist

My mom is one of my biggest cheerleaders. We took a quick picture at a mother's day brunch that I spoke at in Northwest Arkansas. I love this lady!

Sharing God's Word in Springfield, Missouri.

CHAPTER 30

Saying Goodbye to The American Dream

One summer, my parents gave us tickets for a trip to an amusement park in Hot Springs, Arkansas. We arrived at the park and paid for parking. I knew we couldn't afford the food in the park because our budget was still so tight. We decided to eat an early lunch in the car, and I had plenty of snacks to take into the park with us. We walked into the park and rode a few rides. We walked around and watched Jake and Andrew take it all in.

A couple of hours into our day, Jake asked for an ice cream cone. I told him that I had snacks in my bag and that he could have one of those. He didn't throw a fit but just took the fruit snacks that I brought and ate them. I looked around at all the other kids in the park, and the tears started welling up in my eyes. I wanted more than anything to give Jake and Andrew an ice cream cone, a funnel cake, and a big stuffed animal.

"Lord, help me to be thankful," I prayed. Less than five minutes later, a vendor walked up to our family and asked if it was OK to give Jake and Andrew an ice cream cone. She had no idea about our situation, and she had no idea Jake had just asked for one. I was speechless.

For years, we had sacrificed, scrimped, and saved to start True Vine Ministry. We had lived on a tight budget so that our family could serve in ministry. We worked hard to make every dollar count. It was hard work, and sometimes it felt pointless. The question, *Where was the blessing of God?*" was asked in my head and in my heart more times than I could count.

But God. He was teaching our family about His real blessing and His real favor and how it doesn't necessarily have to do with finances and certainly has everything to do with Him! Although it was sometimes hard to see, the tight budget became one of the best ways God showed His faithfulness to us because He creatively provided everything we needed.

I learned to embrace the tight budget and started to look for "grace gifts" each day. These were special ways that God showed up and showed out. It could be as simple as the meat that I needed to buy being on sale or the light staying "green" because I was running late for a meeting. God taught us how to live for Him. He provided in more ways than we could know.

Our tight budget lasted for ten long years. (TEN LONG YEARS!) I know that ten years doesn't seem like long, unless you are in the middle of it. While it was hard, it was a necessary span of time. The desire to live the American dream was deeply rooted in me. I had longed for it and planned for it most of my life.

When our bank account grew enough for luxuries like home renovations, I was excited but for a different reason. On renovation day, we gathered a crew of people to help us. One of the first things we tackled was our pink Pepto-Bismol carpet.

A few of us went around the sides of the room and loosened up the carpet so it would come up easily. As I was ripping out the carpet, tears started to flow. I wasn't crying because of the decade of pink carpet, and it wasn't just tears of joy for the hardwood I had dreamed about. I was rejoicing and thanking God for the work He had done in my life. I had come to accept and even be thankful for the pink carpet. God was reminding me that He had provided us a home. He had provided us with everything we needed, and He had taught me to embrace it and be thankful for it. God had truly done a miracle in my life, and the miracle wasn't that we were getting new hardwood floors. The miracle was that God had changed my heart.

The American dream had been my goal. After ten years of living with pink carpet and flowered wallpaper, the goal had changed. And in the process, God had provided tiny blessings that meant more to me than anything a full bank account could have provided—things like ice cream cones in a small amusement park in central Arkansas.

The question that plagued my life ten years earlier was finally answered: "Where was the blessing and favor of God?" It turns out that it was there all the time—in His moment-by-moment presence in my life. I learned that God works in deeper ways than what we can comprehend. God was in fact blessing our lives even though our bank account was usually running on empty. I was slowly learning to allow God to chart the direction of my life. He used Pepto-Bismol carpet and flowered wallpaper to teach me about His real blessing and favor.

As I ripped the pink carpet out of our house, I praised God for His goodness. I worshipped Him as every inch of that carpet came up. Then we loaded the pink carpet into the bed of my dad's truck and took it to the dump. I tossed it in the landfill and with it I tossed the need to live for the American dream.

CHAPTER 31

Life with Andrew

As Andrew grew up, his personality took shape. He was an easygoing, laid-back, kind of kid who was happy to be at home and to be with his family. When it was time for him to start school, he jumped in there and made friends. Andrew and Jay are a lot alike. They don't need to be the center of attention, but they both have "rock" personalities: They're strong, they're loyal, they're stable, and they're always consistently there for you.

When Andrew was eight, he started asking questions about God and Heaven and Jesus. We saw the Lord working in his life, but he never said anything about asking Jesus into his heart. I was so worried about that, and I didn't know if I should encourage him to pray a prayer or not. Jay and I prayed and prayed. We didn't want to force anything, but we didn't want to be too laid-back about it either.

Finally, we called Andrew into our bedroom one day and asked him, "Do you want to be saved?" It really was that simple. And Andrew said, "YES! I want to ask Jesus into my heart." In his own words, Andrew prayed the sweetest prayer. That night, Jake said, "Andrew, tonight I am sleeping in your room because we are brothers in a brand new way." My heart melted. The next week, Andrew proudly shared his decision to follow Jesus with our church family. Jay, Andrew, Jake, and I stood at the front of the sanctuary at church and hundreds of people came by and hugged our necks. I cried the entire time. I was so thankful to know that both of my boys knew Jesus. It was a relief that made perfect sense once I experienced it. I traveled all over Arkansas and beyond and told women about Jesus, but there was something so special about telling my own son about Him. And then I was able to see Jesus work in his heart and save him. Nothing, and I do mean nothing, is as special as that!

Andrew doesn't demand a lot of attention or things. When I want to buy him something, he usually says, "Oh, no, Mom, we don't need to spend that money." Or "I don't need that. I'm fine; I've got plenty." He did go through a phase when he was about five or six when he kept asking for a dog, but I kept saying, "No!" I was sure that we didn't need another mouth to feed!

Then one month I decided to go on a hike with my friend Janet. Her husband, Mark, was our pastor at the time, and Janet is one of my close friends and my accountability partner. She loved—and loves—to go backpacking.

The way she does it, you put everything that you need to survive on your back, and you go into the backcountry, off the beaten path, and you hike and set up camp where there's no running water or commodes along the way. You filter your water from the stream so you have water to drink, cook your food on a campfire, and go to the bathroom in the woods—it's roughing it! And it's not my thing, but Janet had asked me to go with her for years. Finally, she said, "Which weekend works for you? We're going to do this."

She had written a manual of instructions and supplies. I was reading the manual and talking to the kids about it. "Oh, I need to be sure to exercise and be in shape so I can walk on these hills and valleys and trails. And then there's this section about what to do to avoid bears, because we have bears here in Arkansas. I don't need to put on deodorant, I don't need to wear any kind of smelly lip gloss, I need to be careful about the scents of lotions I wear, and I need to put my food in Ziploc bags so the bear can't smell it ... ."

In her manual, she also talked about how backpackers "bear-bag." Before sleeping, they take their food and put it about half a mile away so if the bear goes to anything, it will go to the food and not to the backpacker. I also told the boys, "I want you to know I'm going to follow these rules. And I'm also memorizing some 'bear Scripture.' If I see a bear, I'm just going to speak truth into that bear's life!"

Over the years, I have tried to model a life that follows Jesus so that my boys can see me living out my faith. Anytime I memorize Scripture, I tell my boys what I am memorizing and in what area of life the passage equips me. Whether that's a possible bear encounter, a situation at work, or friendships, God's Word is relevant in all circumstances.

Andrew was watching and processing all of my preparations for the hike. Somewhere in his mind, he decided that the one thing standing in the way of him getting a dog was me. And just maybe that bear was going to be the answer! So one day he said, "Mom, when you go on your hike with Mrs. Janet, if a bear eats you, can I get a dog?"

I told him, "Honey, that bear's not going to eat me. I'm going to follow all the rules, and I have my 'bear Scripture,'" and he repeated, "I'm just saying, if that bear eats you, can we get a dog?" I told him, "Listen, if the bear eats me, tell your dad that I said you could get TWO dogs."

He walked around the corner of the house and was out of sight, so he didn't know that I could still hear him. "Yes!" he exclaimed.

I called Jay and said, "We have to get a dog because Andrew is throwing me to the bears around here!" So we did. We ended up getting a Maltese named Lulu, a little princess dog. I laugh because while Jay, Andrew, and Jake all wanted a dog and I didn't, I'm the one who got the dog. Lulu has attached herself to me, and I'm the center of her universe.

When we picked up Lulu, Andrew looked at her and said, "Hi. I'm going to be your dad, and you can call me Mr. Andrew." "Oh my gosh," I thought, "he has always been the baby. He has never had anybody to boss or correct. This is going to be so good for him, and we are going to have to keep this dog forever!" Andrew does love that dog and is very loyal to Lulu. Lulu has been a big part of our family, and Andrew is the reason why we have her.

Andrew has been easy to parent. Like me, he follows the rules. Sometimes I have to help him not be too laid-back, but in the process, he helps me not to be too high-strung. Andrew's personality from the time he was born invited me to be still and to simply enjoy being a mom. "Calm down, Mom, everything is going to be OK," regularly comes out of his mouth. I am forever grateful for the blessing of Andrew. He has taught me how to love life and to embrace each day with thankfulness, contentment, and a deep peace in my heart for God's perfect plan.

Andrea and Andrew!

Andrew and Jake spent many hours on the tire swing.

Andrew loves to hunt and fish!

Andrew's first day of school! Both boys went to Jim Stone Elementary in Conway, Arkansas.

Lulu is the queen of our house. Don't tell her she is a dog!

Andrew's big catch!

CHAPTER 32

Arkansas and The Ends of The Earth

One of my favorite devotions in my book *Free To Thrive* talks about my love for boxes, cubbies, and bins. Even when I was in kindergarten, I loved to see a bin that had "Andrea" written on it. In my world, things should have a place and be in their place. I am not a naturally neat or organized person, and I have my fair share of junk drawers, but I do like to keep things categorized in my mind.

As I started True Vine Ministry, I saw myself serving the women of Arkansas and only the women of Arkansas. I remember thinking, "That should be enough for me and for God." I loved my home state of Arkansas and felt safe with "my girls." I was a "Bible Study girl." I never had a desire to travel overseas or to be involved in missions. That was always for others. I wanted to stay close to home and in my "strike zone," where I knew I could do OK. As usual, God had other plans.

My first opportunity to travel overseas and host a women's conference was to Paris, France. I almost hyperventilated. My mind immediately went to all the reasons why it was "not a good time," or "not a good fit," or "not in God's will." I prayed about the opportunity for two minutes before I felt that it was not an option. I was so relieved God didn't ask me to do something so out of my comfort zone.

A couple of years passed, and I was leading a conference for the Arkansas Baptist State Convention. The event was a large-scale event with hundreds of leaders from around the state. In between teaching sessions, I walked down the hall to take a quick bathroom break. I saw my friend Bob Fielding in the hall and mentioned in passing (and with no desire to start a conversation) that I was praying for him and a team he was taking to southeast Europe. Bob stopped walking, looked at me, and asked, "You want to go with us?" I was stunned by the invitation. The team was made up of pastors who would travel to the other side of the world to host a training event for national pastors. Bob said, "You can lead a conference for the women." In the moment, I said the only thing I could say: "I'll pray about it."

Once again, I prayed and had the same "no-go" feeling. Which was good, because the trip was definitely out of my comfort zone. I sent an email to Bob and declined the trip, but this time I decided to be a little more helpful. I gave names of friends to him who would be a great fit for the team.

With the possibility of that trip behind me, I breathed a sigh of relief. About two weeks later, I woke up one morning and prayed, *"Lord, today, wherever you tell me to go, I will go, and whatever you tell me to do, I will do it."* As soon as I voiced the prayer, I thought, "Those are some pretty big words, sister." I shook off a feeling of uneasiness and started my day.

I made breakfast for the boys and fixed Jay's lunch. I dropped Jake and Andrew off at school and came home and turned on my computer. There was an email waiting for me from Bob. He said that he woke up that morning and during his quiet time, felt impressed to give me one more chance at the trip. In that moment, I knew I had to go.

I was a nervous wreck as I made plans to travel to the other side of the world. I felt ill-prepared in every way. I would have to speak through a translator. I would have to try to relate biblical truths to the lives of people I didn't know and had never met. I wasn't sure how I would do any of those things. I was convinced that I wouldn't enjoy the trip and that it was going to be a "one-and-done" experience for me.

The day finally arrived, and there was no turning back. I was going on an overseas mission trip. I looked like a whipped dog by the time we made it from Little Rock to Atlanta, which was only two hours into a twenty-four hour travel day! I was searched in the Paris airport and was in tears by the time we boarded our fourth and final flight of the journey. I didn't sleep a wink during the twenty-four hours of travel.

I wish I could tell you all of the details from the trip because it was amazing. What I can tell you is that my life was forever changed during my time overseas. I fell in love with people from the other side of the world. I saw that their needs are great and that the differences between our cultures are superficial at best. I sat with and taught an amazing group of ladies. I watched God's Word transform their lives.

In the course of one week, I developed lifelong bonds that will never be broken. The women I served were so hungry for the Word. I hadn't seen that type of desperation before. They needed a word from Jesus. Their lives were full of hardship and persecution, like nothing I had ever experienced. Their passion for Jesus moved me and changed me.

My trip overseas flew by and before I knew it, it was time to return to America. On the bus ride to the airport, the pastor of the church where we served sat next to me. He asked me to come back to his country and to bring my family. I told him I would pray about it, and we would stay in touch. He looked at me and asked, "May I share something with you?" "Of course," I said. He said, "If you will let go of control of your life, God will use you in an amazing way. He will give you family all over this world." I looked out the window and thought about what he said for the rest of the ride. I knew God had given the pastor insight into my greatest challenge—letting go of control.

I returned home and resumed my normal schedule. God laid it on Jay's heart to email the pastor. They developed a friendship and, long story short, we returned to that country in a big way. We enlisted the help of our home church, Second Baptist Conway, and other churches in the state of Arkansas and have taken many teams to that part of the world.

My days of thinking, "I am the Bible study girl from Arkansas who will only serve in Arkansas," were over.

Trips to other countries came along, too. I traveled to the Ukraine to help lead several women's conferences. I also traveled to Germany to lead a Bible study for people who live and serve full-time overseas. There have been lots of trips, and most of them I can't discuss, but God started opening doors, and I have seen His work all over His world.

I have to tell you a funny story from my trip to the Ukraine. I traveled with a small team of women to serve as conference leaders at three women's events. I struggled with the decision to go. The trip was during the busiest part of my speaking calendar. I had the eight days open, but the days leading up to the trip and the days following the trip were packed with events. I prayed and felt led to go.

A few days before we were scheduled to leave, Jake came down with a stomach bug. We are notorious for catching stomach bugs in my family, but this was especially bad timing. I managed to rearrange my schedule so I could take care of Jake, and I put off my packing until later. Next came Andrew, and he was as sick as Jake, if not worse. I managed to work my way through the planned events and did everything I could to not get sick myself. By the day before we left, my hands were raw from the number of times I washed them. I finally decided I had to pack, so I stopped doing the "sick people" laundry. I designated one bath tub as the quarantined area for dirty sheets, towels, and clothes. I packed my bag and hopped on the plane.

We flew from Little Rock to Atlanta. We made the long flight from Atlanta to Amsterdam and got ready to board the flight for Kiev. Within a matter of ten minutes, the stomach bug hit. I didn't want anyone to know I was sick, so I did my best to keep it quiet. We landed in Kiev, and as I got off the plane, I grabbed every airplane sickness bag I could find.

Our contacts in the Ukraine scheduled a driver to pick us up and take us on a sightseeing tour of Kiev. We needed to kill several hours before we boarded an overnight train to our final destination. I think I threw up at every major sightseeing spot in that beautiful city. There were tears (lots of tears), and I wanted to go home.

When we boarded the train, and I was able to lie down for the first time in over twenty hours, the fever set in. I was cold and hot at the same time. Covered in chills and sweating like crazy, I endured the long train ride. Eventually we arrived at our final destination.

We were staying in the home of a Ukrainian family. I didn't want to get anyone sick, but there was nothing I could do about the situation. As soon as we settled into our rooms and had a small breakfast, it was time to hit the ground and do our orientation meeting. I was weak and tired. Part of the orientation was going to Freedom Square. We learned about the culture and went to an open-air market. It was cold in Ukraine, so I was wearing a large ski-style coat with Velcro on the front. I went through the motions of looking around the square and shopping while trying hard to stay on my feet. I went into one booth full of clothes and leaned over a table in order to try on a hat.

I visited other booths and wandered for a while before two women stopped me. They were trying to tell me something, but I couldn't understand Ukrainian, and they spoke no English. Finally, they pointed to the front of my coat. When I looked down, I was horrified to see that I had "stolen" a pair of size XXL leopard panties. I hadn't even noticed that the Velcro from my coat had snagged them from the booth. I went to the missionary and told her what happened. She started to laugh. I didn't know what to do. I thought about taking the easy way out, just sending money to the booth and paying for them. We all agreed that I should go back and explain what happened. It wasn't my proudest moment, but being able to laugh about it with people in the booth made for a special memory. Despite the rocky start, the trip went really well.

The lesson I have learned time and time again when it comes to international work is that obstacles will arise. I promise you that someone will get sick, the kids will act up, or your spouse's job will become crazy busy. Satan has a way of trying to throw his fiery darts at us when we are passionately pursuing the gospel. Over time, I have come to expect problems to suddenly crop up. I can't tell you how many times I have claimed, "...the one who is in you is greater than the one who is in this world." (1 John 4:4)

It has been neat to realize that we don't have to travel overseas to have an international ministry opportunity. Jay and I connected with our good friend Ara Torosian in California, where we spent several days with Pastor Ara and his family. Sitting around the table in his home, we caught up on life. Our time together reminded me how I often take my church and religious freedom for granted. Unlike me, he didn't grow up in a church-going family or have a comfortable job as a minister. After coming to faith in Iran and becoming a house church leader, Ara was imprisoned for his faith and discouraged from sharing it with others. When he was released from jail, he came to America to escape persecution.

Ara invited me to speak at his church in Burbank, California. While we were there, God opened up a door for Jay and me to be featured on an international television show that broadcasts in several countries. The show was an hour long. The first thirty minutes, I shared a message of encouragement. The last thirty minutes was a call-in time for people from all over the world. The experience was surreal and amazing. Jay and I got some tough questions. When the really hard questions came in, I would look at Jay and smile. He did a great job answering them! The show was live, so there was no way for us to discuss how to respond. We trusted God to give us His words to share, and He did!

The call to missions is important because once you go, you are never the same. Your values change. Your perspectives change. Your goals change. I'm a firm believer in the fact that if you can go, you should go.

Fear can keep us from getting outside of our comfort zone and enjoying the family of God that is all over this world. The call to take the gospel to the ends of the earth is a serious call. It's a call that is on all of our lives. I think about the times when I believed this call was only for others, and it makes me mad. I missed lots of opportunities because of fear and wanting to be in control. Thankfully, God showed me that His plans are far greater than my boxes, cubbies, and bins.

So fun to visit villages and share God's love on the other side of the world! Notice the cow walking down the street. These people are my people!

I never thought I would leave Arkansas. God had other plans. The Great Wall of China is amazing. The world is a big place and there are so many people to meet and serve.

Sharing God's Word with Ara's church in Burbank, California.

Sharing with a church in Ukraine. Notice the head scarf and no make up.

CHAPTER 33

Struggles

One year, I recruited and led a team of business professionals on an international mission trip. Everyone on the trip was a high-level leader. The team was made up of CEOs, international speakers, international trainers, and community leaders. We all knew each other and went to church together. I was very excited about the trip and the opportunity to connect faith with the business world. For several of the team members, it was their first international mission trip.

The day came for us to leave. At some point in the process, I began to question my ability to lead a group of leaders. I wondered if they would see my insecurities. I wondered if I had the necessary skills to keep the group moving in the same direction. I believed that I was probably the weakest leader on the team. I pushed my uneasiness aside and tried to focus on the task ahead. That was how I handled struggles. I would bury them or try to cover them up with "good things" by getting busier and busier.

On the flight over, I was sitting next to my good friend, mentor, and accountability partner, Donna. I told you about Donna in a previous chapter. She and her husband gave me a set of Bible commentaries during my seminary days. Donna is a Christian therapist. She also does leadership training in the business world. I could write an entire book on Donna and her role in my life. Donna loves Jesus, and she loves others. She has a heart to help people and is extremely gifted in seeing needs and speaking truth into the lives of others.

I remember telling Donna on the flight over, "There is a reason God put this group together. I think we need to challenge everyone to look for the ways God is working in their personal lives during this trip." When I said that to Donna, it was a very real thought, and I meant every word of it. Little did I know how that thought was going to impact me!

Another good friend of mine, Brad Lacy, was on the trip. Brad is like a brother to me, and his parents are like another set of parents. Our families are close. In fact, my kids call him "Uncle Brad." Brad loves to give me a hard time by playing practical jokes and pointing out all the ways I take life too seriously. At the same time,

Brad is loyal and protective. I never have to question his heart toward me or my family. Brad is a great leader and is the CEO of the Conway Area Chamber of Commerce.

One of Brad's favorite memories of me happened years earlier when we were at a church choir Christmas party. There were tons of people at the party and not enough places for everyone to sit. Brad was standing close to me and Jay. At the time, we didn't know him very well. When I saw Brad standing up, I offered to give him my seat. He and Jay both looked at me like I was crazy. "Why would a girl offer a guy her seat?" Now, we laugh about that memory because it's a perfect example of me trying to take care of the people around me to the point that I create an awkward moment for everyone!

Our team arrived at our destination and settled in for a week of work. From the outside, the week went really well. We led a business conference and connected with hundreds of business professionals. We spent time with the local believers and formed strong relationships. God was opening doors, and we were walking through them and seeing God move in a mighty way.

As the week progressed, painful thoughts from my past kept welling up inside of me. I tried to push the thoughts away, but I couldn't. I found myself thinking about my life and all of the things I was unsure about. I was so unsettled in my heart.

Out of the blue one night, I started talking about my adoption and some of the feelings that I associated with my adoption. The men from the team were leading a men's event so it was just me, Donna, and one of our missionary friends. I started to share about the pain I associated with the nursery window from my birth and how hard it was for me. I started to talk about the feelings of isolation and loneliness that had plagued my life. I looked up, and Donna and our friend had tears in their eyes. I realized that I did, too.

One night after that, Donna and I were sitting on our bunk beds in a room that we shared. Donna simply said, "Andrea, if you don't deal with your struggles, it will affect your ministry." That statement got my attention. I always thought I could keep my struggles compartmentalized. I could be the "Bible study" girl who taught and shared God's Word with power and conviction and at the same time, hide my own insecurities, questions, and doubts. And to be honest, both of those realities were true for me. I loved Jesus. I loved His Word. I believed in the power of God to change lives. At the same time, I struggled to believe that all of God's Word was true for me.

I didn't know it at the time, but Donna and Brad were observing my struggles and taking notes. They both knew me well at that point, but I don't think they fully understood the amount of struggle in my life until we were on the trip. I later found out that Brad and Donna were discussing their thoughts about me during the long bus rides between ministry stops. I had no idea the talks were happening; I was just trying to get through the trip and hold it together.

Finally, the week came to an end, and we returned home. I was glad to be back in America and back to my normal routine of family, life, and ministry. I was ready to hit the ground running. As usual, I tried to forget about the hard memories and struggles that were surfacing. It was the summertime, and we had lots of trips and activities planned. I was just going to get busy and stay busy.

My sweet friend Donna Seal. This lady has my heart!

So thankful for the special friendship I share with Donna Seal and Brad Lacy. These two are a picture of God's love and grace in my life.

My good friend and big brother Brad Lacy. This guy is the real deal and so good to me and my family! We call him, "Uncle Brad."

CHAPTER 34

Unexpected Gifts

One day not too long after the mission trip, Donna called me. She had talked to Brad, and they wanted to schedule a time to visit with me. She asked if I would come to her home so the three of us could have lunch. Donna was honest with me; she and Brad wanted to share some of the things they observed on the trip. The invitation was very kind and loving. Donna left the decision up to me. There would be no judgment either way. I told Donna I would think about it.

I knew I needed to talk to Jay and get his thoughts on the situation. Of course, Jay knew about the long-term struggles in my life. He had watched them play out for years. I asked him what he thought about the invitation. Jay and I agreed it was time for me to face my issues and begin to deal with them. The first step was to visit with Donna and Brad and to hear their observations. The next day, I called Donna and set up the lunch.

I have to admit I was relieved when Donna called and asked me to let her and others help me. Deep down, I knew my struggles were real and were deeply affecting me. At the same time, I had no idea what to do with them. I had normalized my behavior and accepted it for many years. I hadn't talked much about my struggles since the day I sat down with my mentor, Jimmie, several years earlier.

The day of the lunch finally arrived. I walked into the house, and Brad and Donna were waiting for me. They gave me a big hug. "It's Andrea day!" I wasn't sure what Donna and Brad were going to share, but I knew I was in a safe place. Being the large-and-in-charge person I am, I walked into Donna's home with a plan. I had done some exploring and examining of my own. I had looked at my tendencies and knew that some of them were not healthy.

We sat down, and I told Donna and Brad that I wanted to lead the discussion. Both of them laughed and said, "Of course you do." I had identified three tendencies in my life that were crippling me. The struggles had been consistently part of my life, but I didn't know how to break the cycle. I had written the three things on a piece of paper and read them off, one by one.

I remember saying, *"I feel like I'm a burden to the people around me. I constantly feel bad for just being present."* Next, I said, *"If anyone ever does anything nice for me, I feel like I have to do something equally nice or even nicer for them. I am so tired of keeping score."* Finally, I said, *"I always feel like I am on the outside. I can't imagine what it's like to be part of a group."* At this point, I felt the weight of my struggles on me. I knew the last one was the biggest problem I had. It was really heavy.

I had accepted these three beliefs as my reality. At the same time, I wanted out. I really did. I continued to talk, and it was clear that I associated all of these feelings with my adoption. That was the easy answer for me. "If I hadn't been adopted, then I wouldn't have any of these struggles."

I asked Donna, "What should I do?" I was desperate for answers and willing to give anything a try. Donna told me exactly what she thought I should do. "Andrea, you have to talk to your parents." Of course, that was the one thing I wasn't willing to do. I didn't want to hurt my parents. I didn't want them to know that I struggled with these feelings. They had been so good to me and had done everything in their ability to love me and provide for me. I didn't want to come across as ungrateful. I was stuck.

Also, fear was controlling my life. I was afraid that once I started looking into my adoption and the details of it, I might uncover more than I could handle. What if there was more to the story than I knew? What if the haunting fears were true? Maybe I wasn't wanted, maybe I wasn't valuable, maybe I wasn't needed!

All of these lies had been in my head for so long. I had never spoken them to anyone. I just tried to make the noise of my life louder than the noise in my head. I stayed busy. I tried to be good and do good. I worked hard to love others.

Donna and Brad could tell I was struggling. Brad looked at me and said, "Andrea, all of your feelings are a paper tiger." I didn't know what he meant, so I asked him to explain. He said, "You think all of these feelings are true, so they are big and threatening to you, but they aren't." We finished our discussion, and I promised to think and pray about my next step. However, I was resolved to find a way to deal with my issues without talking to my parents. I just couldn't go down that path.

Donna had made a delicious lunch for us. She asked Brad to pray before we ate. As Brad prayed, he said something that hit me like a ton of bricks. He said, *"Lord, please help Andrea with these strongholds in her life."* My head popped up as soon as he said it. I don't think anyone had ever told me I had a stronghold in my life. I was willing to admit that I had a few struggles, but calling them strongholds seemed a little extreme. I had always found my identity in being the "spiritual girl." I was the one who had it all together, and I was the one who prayed those types of prayers over others. I didn't say anything about the prayer or how it affected me. At first, I was defensive about it, but somehow I moved past that and decided to tuck the prayer away in my heart so that I could talk to the Lord about it. *"Lord, do I have a stronghold?"* was the question I needed to ask.

I left Donna's house unsure of what I was going to do. Simply speaking the lies out loud was a huge step for me. Saying them forced me to look at them. Saying them brought them out into the light of God and His Word. Once I gave voice to them, they started to lose their control over me. I look back on that day now, and I know it was one of the most transformational days in my life. I spoke the lies out loud, and I started to engage in the spiritual battle of replacing them with truth.

After I came home from Donna's house, I quickly loaded my car and drove to a speaking engagement that was happening that night. I was scheduled to teach my "Free To Thrive" Bible study to a group of ladies. As I drove to the event, I prayed and asked God to help me. I couldn't get away from the idea of having a stronghold in my life. The paradox of Donna and Brad praying that over me and then me teaching on freedom a few hours later was not lost on me. The need to be in control and the desire to live by faith had always been constant companions to me. I wanted both of them. As a result, this tug of war raged inside of me.

I arrived at the event and parked my car. I set up my book table, visited with the ladies, and prepared to teach. I did my best to shake off the events from my day and focus on the Lord and serving His people.

That night, I taught Galatians 5:1. I was a little teary eyed as I taught. I imagine that I needed the message of Jesus' freedom more than anyone else at the event. As I taught, I heard myself say something that nearly stopped me in my tracks. I said, "Ladies, why would we settle for less than God's best? God purchased our freedom, and He offers it to us today. We need to do whatever is necessary to stand in the freedom that He graciously provides!"

Afterward, I drove home and told Jay about my day. We both agreed I had to follow Donna's advice. I needed to share my feelings and thoughts with my parents. I picked up the phone and called my Mom and Dad. It was 10:00 p.m., and they were probably a little alarmed when I told them I would be making the two-hour drive the next morning so that I could be at their house for lunch. I assured them I was fine but needed to talk.

When I walked into my parents' house, I could smell the roast that was cooking. It was the smell of home. Mom, Dad, and I held hands and prayed around the table. I shared what was going on in my life. I talked about the nursery window and how I had felt alone at different times in my life. I asked questions I had always wanted to ask, and they gave me every detail they knew. It was a special and freeing time. One thing was sure in my heart and mind following the conversation: the lies that had been running around in my head were not my reality. At least they didn't have to be. I wasn't a burden to my family, I didn't have to pay them back for the kindness they extended to me, and I wasn't on the outside!

I drove back to Conway with a peace in my heart and a deep sense of gratitude resting all over my life. As I drove, I thought about my conversation the day before with Donna and Brad. I was overwhelmingly thankful for their honesty. I had been a little defensive, and I had wanted to be in control, but they handled me with love. They told me the truth because that's what friends do. They challenged me, encouraged me, and provided a safe place for me to explore the deep pain that had been in my life for so many years. I knew they would be so excited to hear about my conversation with my parents.

When I pulled into my driveway, I was surprised to find an unexpected gift next to my front door. It was a houseplant and had a card attached that read, "Happy Friend Day." The card was signed, "Your Secret Friend."

For the next four months, a gift would show up every few weeks on my doorstep or in my mailbox. I received gift cards, a monogrammed cup, a cute clipboard, and a painting. God was at work in my life, using someone who had no idea what I was dealing with to encourage me. Through God's constant love, the truth of His Word, my mystery friend's gifts, my parents' unconditional love, and the support of others, I slowly started to accept the truth: *I wasn't a burden to others, I didn't have to pay people back for a kindness they extended to me, I wasn't stuck on the outside of every group or relationship, and*

there were people who loved and accepted me for me.
What an unexpected gift!

I was thankful for God's perfect timing and how all of
the conversation happened at just the right time and in
just the right way. I was especially thankful I was able
to tell my parents how much I love them and how they
have always been and will always be my Mom and Dad.
They are my gift! They ground me, support me, love me,
and provide for me in so many different ways.

Satan is a liar, and his plan is to steal, kill, and destroy
our lives. He will lie to you, just like he lied to me. But,
we don't have to live in the lie. Freedom comes in knowing, believing, and trusting the truth. Jesus said it best:
The truth always sets us free.

CHAPTER 35

Friendships

When God works in one area of your life, get ready! His work will often start to affect other areas, too. Once I started to deal with the struggles that came from the three lies I believed about myself, I started to see how those lies were affecting everything. One of the main areas was my friendships.

Friendship had always been a big deal for me. (Remember when we moved to Conway, and I had the three-step process for making friends?) I've always wanted to fill my life with lots of friends. But I've also always had this caution when it came to friendships. I wanted to avoid letting them get too close to me. I've tried to stay in control, making sure that I'm not over-investing or underinvesting with others. If I was over-investing, I was vulnerable because I gave the other person the ability to reject me, which would break my heart. If I was under-investing, I was constantly worried that I wasn't doing enough to earn and keep their friendship.

These extremes produced a cycle in my friendships, and the cycle became a controlling factor in my life. I would run into a friendship and hope and believe that maybe, finally, this would be the friendship I was looking for. The friendship that would fill the emptiness in my heart. I would jump in, full force, and for a season— maybe a year or two—I would be all about that friend. Then I would find myself slowly pulling back as a wall started going up in my heart.

I can look back now and see how that was a defense mechanism. I wanted to leave them before they had the chance to leave me. I worried they could only handle me, or my family, for a certain amount of time. I would constantly be trying to gauge, "Have I stayed too long? Have I not stayed long enough?" I was in constant turmoil. I wanted the friendships, but I wasn't healthy enough to have them. I would work so hard to do everything right so I could earn my way into a person's life. Then, whenever I had the chance to be involved in their life, I was scared and would pull back.

If I ever sensed that somebody was upset with me or that our friendship was changing, I would find a way to leave the friendship or redefine the relationship in a new direction. I wanted to be in control and make sure I didn't get hurt. It was important to me that my heart never got too vulnerable.

Then, I met a group of friends who recognized the struggles going on inside of me and who literally wouldn't let me go. (Donna, Brad, and so many others were a part of this group!) We were close for a while, but then I started to pull back. I tried so hard to run from them. I would decide to no longer be friends, but that didn't work. I tried to redefine the relationships with new rules. I resolved to only talk to them at church or every other week. I tried to refuse to go on the next trip or lunch outing. I tried so hard not to engage, and they just graciously wouldn't have it!

They held on to me, they held on to my family, and God put us in situations and circumstances where it was clear we were going to be in one another's lives. Through that, I found a beautiful picture of love, devotion, and fighting for someone, even when they aren't quite sure they need to fight for themselves.

I'm so thankful for the fact that my friendship journey has brought me to a new place of recognizing that God, in His goodness and grace, ordains, allows, and calls people to be in our lives. There are people who notice us. People who love us. People who want to be in our lives. And, it's our opportunity to accept them and to let them be in our lives. When we do, our lives are richer and more meaningful than when we were alone.

Friendships can and do change. Is life always easy when it comes to friendships? No! Are there ups and downs? Yes! Are there times when our friendships transition or are redefined? Absolutely! But when we are at a healthy place, we're able to roll with it. Friendship has definitely been a journey for me, but it's been a good journey. I now have an extended "family" of friends, and I know they're going to be a part of my life, for the rest of my life.

My group is the most unexpected group I could imagine, but I know God picked them for me. We have so many crazy moments and moments where I think, "This is like a big dysfunctional family!" But it's a family that is solid, it's a family that is devoted, and it's a family that is real and authentic to the core.

A new friend rhythm has been established in my life. Instead of the cycle of over-investing and underinvesting, there's a refreshing sense of steadiness. That's not to say that I don't have setbacks, falling into old thought patterns or behaviors; I do. But I'm noticing that they happen less and less often.

New behaviors have taken the place of the old ones. Worries and tensions have been gradually replaced with peace. I feel free to do fun things like spending the holidays together, Sunday lunches after church, summer vacations, and big meals with plenty of stories to share.

One thing that has become a tradition is playing dominoes. It's not uncommon for me to return home from a speaking engagement, throw on some casual clothes, and then head out with my family to meet up with friends for dominoes and dinner.

I love to play games, and I'm very competitive. I've always thought of myself as a good domino player. I try not to get all worked up, but I can usually only get through one round calmly. After that, I'm either super excited because I'm winning or super frustrated because I'm losing.

When we play dominoes, we have a traditional reciting of the scores, but the reciting of the scores doesn't begin until I'm in last place or next to last place. My friends think it's funny to see me go from extremes of "I'm conquering this game!" to "I hate this game! Why are we playing it? It's just a waste of time!" The kids are called in, and the fun begins: "Bringing up the rear is Andrea, with 326 points." It's a production that gets me worked up no matter how spiritual I try to be!

Freedom comes when we settle into life and live it for the glory of God. My life is full of people who love me. I'm sure of that. My family and my friends are the best. Yes, they like to give me a hard time by lovingly making fun of me. Why do they get away with it? Because they are loyal to the core. They cheer with me when life is good, and they cry with me when life is hard.

God made us to be in relationship with Him and others. For many years, I was afraid to let others in. Then something changed, and God sent people into my life who wouldn't take no for an answer. And, even though I didn't want to or plan to let them into my life, I took the leap of faith. I am forever blessed and changed because of it!

Beach vacation with friends! Yes, everyone stayed in the same house. Orange Beach, Alabama.

Beach Vacation with friends in Destin, Florida. Summer of 2012.

We raised our babies together and now they are graduating from High School. (April Kinley, Jennifer Glover.)

Some of my favorites in this picture! We sing together, pray together, and enjoy life together. (Jennifer, Melanie, me, and Holli)

Janet Dance and I following a Pastor Date Night at Cross Church in Northwest Arkansas. I am so thankful for the friendship of Mark and Janet Dance.

My sweet friend Lacie Thomas.

CHAPTER 36

Learning to Breathe

For most of my life, I felt like everything was closing in on me. I felt like my life was out of control. I didn't trust God or His plan. I worked hard to be close to people—but not too close. I cycled through friendships and stayed busy. Really busy. I didn't want to look at or deal with my struggles. All the while, God was faithfully paving the way. He was allowing me to get to the end of *me* and *my ways* so I would ultimately want *Him* and *His ways*. I will always be grateful for the fact that God taught me how to breathe. Simply breathe.

Learning how to breathe was a long process. God took me on a journey to get to a place of peace with my past. I had pushed my struggles down, and I had tried to cover them up by being good and doing good things. I didn't know what else to do. All the while, the lies of the enemy were running around in my head and impacting my journey. I think the same thing happens to other Christians all the time. We try to just be good; we try to stay busy and keep moving ahead, and we don't even realize that the lies of the enemy are impacting us.

Most of the time, no one challenges us to stop and deal with what's going on inside of us. That's where the local church can fail to live in authentic community with one another. We don't look one another in the eyes and ask, "Why are you having this struggle in your life? Why do you feel that way? Why are you doing those things?" Instead, we just plan another Bible study or host another event. I don't say that to be judgmental; I did that for years. I just tried to move forward, but what I didn't realize was that it was like I was trying to move forward while carrying hundreds of pounds of extra weight.

My friends changed the status quo when they challenged me to deal with the three lies I had believed all of my life. Once I started, it was like finally stopping and asking God to strip away all the extra weight I had been carrying for so long. I finally stopped "doing" things, and I started asking, *"God, do this work in me! Free me from this weight—this shame and this guilt and this need to constantly be busy so that I feel valued or needed or loved."* Once I started praying that prayer, my life changed.

Instead of doing things so I could feel right, I realized God had already made me right through Jesus. Because of that, I was freed up to do things for Him. I had known this equation my entire life. I could teach it to you with great conviction. However, there came a moment when I had to ask Jesus to help me walk in this equation every single moment of every single day. *The equation of grace. I was loved and valued and wanted and redeemed, not because of me, but because of Him.* I started to live that truth out each day, and the outcome was so sweet. I was able to rest in Him, to love Him, to live for Him, and to know that no matter what happened to me or through my ministry, God was my greatest treasure. He was my treasure, and that had nothing to do with what I did or didn't do for Him or anyone else.

The process of learning to breathe took time. God did the work, but I had to surrender to it. My struggles had layers, which I think is true for all of us. When I would deal with one issue, it would uncover another one. That was OK because once I started to breathe, I didn't want anything else except the love of God. The grace of God. The freedom of Christ. That was what I wanted and needed every single day. The people around me loved me and wouldn't let me settle for less than God's best. They spoke truth into my life, stayed engaged in the process, and wouldn't let go of me.

There's so much value in doing the work and getting rid of the weight. Stopping and saying, "OK, I'm going to get to the core of what's going on in my life. I'm going to ask God to change me so that I can move forward without shame, guilt, and doubt. I'm going to ask God to show me the lies running around in my head."

I believe deeply that we don't have to live in guilt and bondage; we don't have to live in shame and doubt. We really can experience the freedom of Jesus Christ. The freedom of knowing that He loves us. The freedom of knowing that He has a plan for our lives. And the freedom of knowing that, at the end of the day, He is more than enough for any situation we face.

So many things changed in my life when I simply focused on Jesus and started to breathe. I experienced His healing as I learned to walk daily in His grace. I was a better wife, a better mom, my friendships were deeper, and the focus of my ministry completely changed. The statement that Donna shared with me when we were on our overseas mission trip rang true. "Andrea, if you don't deal with your struggles, it will affect your ministry." Boy, was she right! My struggles were impacting my ministry in ways I didn't even realize.

Before I dealt with my struggles, I looked to my ministry for meaning, purpose, value, and acceptance. True Vine was how I was going to make MY mark on this world. As a result, I would look at ministry opportunities and size them up in the following way: "What can I do? Will people accept me? How will I be perceived? Am I spiritually good enough to help others? Is the quality of my material going to be meaningful to them? Did I make an impact?" I often thought when presented with an opportunity, "I can't do that. That is too big or too much for me."

Once I dealt with my struggles, the way I looked at ministry and measured success changed. My tendency to run from my calling happened less and less. I stopped filtering things (as much) through the lens of myself, and I learned to embrace opportunities differently. I slowly started trusting God by asking Him, "OK, God, is this the right time to do this or do that? Is this Your plan? Does this honor You?" God changed my focus when He brought people into my life and said, "Love them, serve them, and enjoy life with them. That's all I want you to do." I realized I didn't need to worry if I was an effective communicator or had the best three spiritual points for their lives. Instead, I started sharing life with others and fully relying on God for direction. This realization was huge in my life. When I was focused on Him, His plans were driving me. When I was focused on me, my plans and insecurities were holding me back.

Breathing is good. It's necessary. I am a big fan of it, both physically and spiritually. I've learned that it's hard to breathe when you are carrying extra weight. My extra weight was real, and it shaped the direction of my life. Thankfully, God is bigger. He stripped away my need to "do" and my fear of "doing," and He taught me how to breathe. Simply breathe.

Sharing God's Word in Glasgow, Kentucky. God was teaching me and then giving me the opportunity to teach others.

Sweet friends that span many years of life and ministry together. So thankful for Autumn Hardin and Janet Dance.

CHAPTER 37

Adventures in Writing

My first adventure in writing began several years ago when I was asked to serve as the monthly spiritual columnist for *Women's Inc.,* a publication of our local newspaper. Recently I joined the team of another magazine in central Arkansas called *Faulkner Lifestyle.* The magazines are delivered to homes and businesses around the community. I share the gospel, tell stories from my life, and do my best to encourage people in their relationship with God.

Every time I write a column, I'm aware that some of the people who will read it may never step foot in a church. They will casually look through the magazine while sitting in a doctor's office or waiting for their car to be serviced. Maybe the title of my column catches their attention, and they are willing to take a moment to read it. It excites me that God works in the little details of life. I firmly believe that He places the message on my heart each month and uses that message to encourage others, maybe when they least expect it.

When I was in my second year of full-time speaking, I developed a forty-five-minute teaching session based on Romans 12:2. I called the session "Reflecting His Glory." I noticed that the session connected with every audience no matter if I was in Arkansas or on the other side of the world.

One day, at the end of a retreat, a lady said to me, "Every woman needs to hear that message. How can I get the material so I can share it with my friends?" My honest answer was, "You can't."

The following weekend, I led a retreat and taught the same material on Romans 12:2. My good friend Jennifer Glover attended the event. She told me, "Andrea, you need to write a book." I didn't know what to do with that statement. I was certain that I couldn't write a book. The following Monday, I seriously prayed about it. I remember getting on my knees and asking the Lord to show me His plan.

Within thirty minutes, I had written down the table of contents for the book and mapped out every lesson title. I was stunned as I looked at the piece of paper. There was no doubt God had provided direction. I prayed over that piece of paper and trusted God to show me how to write a book.

One by one, I wrote each lesson. It took three years to write and publish *Reflecting His Glory: From Conformity to Transformation*. There was one moment in the process that I'll never forget. I told God that writing was too hard for me and that I couldn't do it. My conversation with the Lord was very similar to the conversation I had years ago with my parents after their meeting with Cookie. "I can't do this. I'm trying so hard, but it doesn't make any difference!"

In the Lord's gentle way, He reminded me ... *We've been here before, and we'll be here again. I got you through it once; I'll get you through it again.* I can't tell you how many times I have needed to be reminded of that. He also reminded me of the other lessons He had taught me along the way: Life isn't always easy, hard work is necessary, success is not guaranteed on the first try, and our character is refined though adversity. As a result, even when I thought I wasn't making any progress, progress was being made. God was with me, and He was making a way.

When I was nearing the end of writing *Reflecting His Glory*, I had no idea what I was going to do with the manuscript. I wrote the book because I was trying to be faithful to God, but I didn't know the next step. The process of taking something on my computer and transforming it into a book that could be read by others seemed impossible. I mean, really—how do you publish a book?

It so happened that I was given the opportunity to travel to Western Europe and lead a Bible study for people serving overseas. During a break between sessions, I struck up a conversation with someone I hadn't met yet. "What do you do?" he asked. I briefly told him about True Vine Ministry. He asked if I had published any resources. (I am blonde and still didn't "get" what God was doing.) I said, "Funny you should ask. I just wrote a book, but I have no idea what to do with it." He smiled and told me and Jay about his publishing company and how he felt led to help new authors break into the publishing world. Jay and I were so thankful for God's gracious leadership in our lives. David Phillips was my first publisher, and he led me through the tricky world of publishing. David connected me with an amazing editor, illustrator, and formatter, all of whom have become invaluable team members at True Vine Ministry.

Even as newbies to the world of publishing, Jay and I had high expectations for my published resources. We wanted the book(s) to have the same quality as something from a large publishing house. God provided the team to make that happen.

Reflecting His Glory was a long writing project that left me feeling empty. The kind of empty that you feel when you have given it your all. The kind of empty that forces you to examine your own life and ask the tough questions. For three years, I poured my life into the project, and I was forced to deal with my own issues of conforming to the American dream along the way.

I took a few months off from writing and spent time with the Lord in prayer. I needed Him to fill my life with a fresh word. I could feel myself getting antsy for my next writing project. Because of my personality, it's hard for me to sit still and not have a project or two going on at the same time. I started reading some of my old *Women's Inc.* columns and noticed that several of them had a common theme of freedom.

I knew I needed a resource that offered a quick bite of spiritual meat and provided a good entry point for women who had never had a quiet time. I started to brainstorm ideas, still unsure about the direction. I often say, "The book tells me what it's supposed to be." I know this sounds strange, but it's true. I collected all the freedom columns from *Women's Inc.* into one place and started filling in the blanks. Once again, I put together a table of contents and started writing. *Free To Thrive: 40 Power-packed Devotions for Women on the Go* was born. And it was surprising to see the project completed in less than one year. One day, I opened an email from my editor that said, "Congratulations, you have birthed another book baby." I was thrilled!

As soon as *Free To Thrive* was published, the ABN (Arkansas Baptist News) Magazine did a feature story on the book. My friends David and Renee Bond saw the article. I received a call from Renee asking me to meet for lunch. Renee served as the women's ministry leader at Geyer Springs First Baptist Church in Little Rock. Geyer has a full media ministry complete with a recording studio.

At lunch, Renee made an unbelievable offer to me. She was nervous as she asked if I would like to record a teaching series on DVD to complement *Free To Thrive*. Renee was upfront that she would have to get approval for the project, but she was so excited about the possibility. I sat in the restaurant and held back tears. I couldn't believe the offer, which was beyond generous. If I had contacted a studio and set up the plans Renee shared with me, the price would have been off the charts. I had to believe that God was opening another door for me and True Vine Ministry.

The taping of the *Free To Thrive* DVDs stretched me. There were microphones, multiple cameras, a live studio audience, a staged set, and bright lights. When I started getting overwhelmed during filming, I told myself to just look at the sweet ladies in the room and teach them the Word of God. The filming took place over a six-week period, and I was so thankful when it was all over! It was a great experience but definitely one that stretched me.

The media team at Geyer Springs took care of editing the material and gave me the files on a disc. Then it was time to figure out how to publish it as a DVD. I heard about a publishing company in New Jersey. It was a secular company but one with a good reputation.

One day I told my boys that I had to make an important phone call, so I went to my bathroom and closed the door. (Doesn't everybody hide in the bathroom when making an important call?) While thinking through what I would say, I decided to keep the specifics of my project to myself. I wasn't going to tell the representative that I was a Bible teacher, and I wasn't going to explain that my material was Bible teaching. It wasn't that I was embarrassed or ashamed, but I thought a business approach would be best. I was going to present myself as a professional communicator who had some material that I wanted to share with my clients. Short and simple. Neat and clean.

God must have been smiling when He saw me trying to follow my plan. I wasn't ten minutes into my "professional" conversation with the representative when she stopped me and asked, "Are you a Christian?" "Ah, yes," I replied carefully. She asked, "Do you teach the Bible?" "Yes." "I'm a Christian, too!" she exclaimed. "And I love doing Bible studies with my friends!" I was so relieved and told her the full story of my project. I even confessed to her that I was a wife and mom and was currently hiding in my bathroom so my kids wouldn't interrupt our important conversation. We both laughed!

After that phone call, my new friend helped me through the publishing process of the DVDs and went above and beyond to make sure my project was handled with care.

Once again, there were hard moments. Publishing a DVD is much different than publishing a book. There were times when I would have to get up from my computer and take a walk around the block. Jay stepped in several times and helped the process move forward.

One special day, the DVD arrived at my house, and I put it in my DVD player. When I saw myself on the screen, sharing God's Word with women, I was speechless. My mind flashed back to my sixteen-year-old self when I watched Kay Arthur teach the Bible. I thought about the moment when God told me, "Andrea, I am preparing you to teach the Bible, too." As I watched myself on television, teaching the Bible, my heart was overwhelmed in a good way. God had been so patient with me. He had been so loving as I ran from His calling. He never gave up on me, even when I gave up on myself.

Just as I was able to give a sigh of relief at having the DVD project behind me, God nudged me in a new direction. After writing *Reflecting His Glory* and *Free to Thrive*, I attended a national speakers and writers conference. I had the chance to meet agents and publishers. One of the agents encouraged me to write a third book.

As soon as I left that meeting, I slipped into a breakout session that was in progress and sat near the back. The lady presenting the session was a published author. She was sharing tips and her personal journey in the publishing world. Then she made a statement that hit me like a ton of bricks. She said, "I have always written out of my strengths. This book was written out of my weakness." I thought about what she said, and it spoke to me. Oftentimes, we write about the areas of our lives where we have victories or successful experiences. This author was saying that she wrote a book out of an area where she was struggling, an area of brokenness. I loved that idea. I wasn't sure why it hit me so hard, but I knew my next book would deal with my struggles in a personal way.

Around that time, several ladies used the *Reflecting His Glory* Bible study and gave me some great feedback. I had written two lessons in that study based on the life of Ruth. It was clear that people wanted to hear more about Ruth. And this wasn't the first time I'd been asked to share more teaching on the life of Ruth, but it was the first time I felt God nudging me to listen. The outcome of these requests was a new book: *On the Road with Ruth: Faith for the Journey.*

I started to research Ruth, Naomi, Boaz, and the kinsmen-redeemer process. I dug around in the Old Testament for several months. I was listening for the Lord to give me clear direction. I couldn't decide if the book was going to be a workbook, devotion, or chapter book. I felt stuck having lots of material to share but not knowing which direction to take.

God is true to His work in our lives. I did face areas of weakness and struggle as I wrote about Ruth. It was during this writing project that I had to deal with the three lies that impacted my life: *The idea of being a bur-*

den to others, the belief that I had to pay a kindness back with an equal or greater kindness, and the feeling of always being on the outside.

Geyer Springs First Baptist Church stepped up once again and offered to record a DVD to complement *On the Road with Ruth.* The entire media team was on board for the second round of tapings. I was excited, too. One of my favorite funny stories happened during a taping segment. One day I went to the studio and recorded video bumpers for the beginning and ending segments of each teaching session. It was an unusually busy day when I was recording the segments. I had stayed up late the night before writing the bumpers. I had to email them to the media team so they could load them to the teleprompter.

First thing in the morning, I went to the salon for hair and makeup. My regular stylist was not available, so she asked her friend to work me in to her schedule. She did. As I was leaving, the stylist said, "I'm going to let you do the eyeliner and mascara so it will be fresh for the recording later. Don't forget!" "No problem," I assured her.

I drove to Little Rock and had a quick meeting with another women's ministry leader. I arrived at the church and went to the studio. I put on all the microphone packs and sat down in front of the camera. I did a test run and was ready to shoot the bumpers. I taped the first one and then asked to watch the playback. I felt like something was off, but I couldn't put my finger on it. I fluffed my hair and decided to retape the bumper. When you tape a bumper, you have to shoot it three times from three different angles. I was reading from a teleprompter, so I had to concentrate to read the material.

I finished the taping and left the church. I drove home and went straight to my church for a meeting and choir rehearsal. After church, I went to the grocery store because that is like my second home. I made it home around nine that night and picked up the house. Around eleven, I went to the bathroom to brush my teeth and wash my face. It was at that moment that it hit me. I never put the eyeliner and mascara on! It totally slipped my mind.

As I was taking my makeup off, I dealt with the fact that I had recorded six video bumpers with heavy makeup but no eyeliner or mascara. I laughed so hard at myself. The next day I told Jay, "This is why speakers have assistants and 'people.' I can't remember all the details. I don't need people, but I could use at least one 'person' to keep an eye on things!" You can check out the videos on my website and see the awkward makeup job for yourself!

My latest release is the book you are currently reading, *God in the Window*. One day I was sitting at home thinking about the encouragement that I give to women. "Know your story, own your story, and share your story." I encourage women to notice how God has worked in the past, how God is working in the present, and have faith that God will continue to work in the future. Have you ever noticed that sometimes the hardest advice to take is our own?

I sat down and started to type. I wrote out the table of contents and was surprised when I had more than thirty chapter titles. I started to write, and once I did, I couldn't stop. *God in the Window* was in fully developed manuscript form in the course of three short weeks. I'm not sure I took a shower or talked to my family in that time. I simply wrote and wrote and wrote. It was so good for me to stop all of my activities and think about my journey with the Lord.

Once the manuscript was complete, I sent it to the editor and focus group. The content was coming along, so it was time to contact my illustrator so she could design the book cover. I'm blessed to work with the best team. They are not people who I hire; they are people who pour their hearts and lives into my projects. I always trust God to work through the team to help the book become what it's supposed to be.

I knew the book cover had to be right. *God in the Window* was a special project that would always have a special place in my heart. The first few covers that were designed were cute but didn't resonate with me. I was so unsettled about the cover and how to communicate the concept of God being in the window of our lives.

Then I remembered something so special. On the last day my friend and mentor Jimmie Sheffield served as interim pastor of Second Baptist Jacksonville, he gave me a gift. It was a copy of the Billy Graham picture that had been on the wall at the Arkansas Baptist State Convention. I rushed to my closet and found the picture. I took it to a local copy shop and asked them to scan it for me. I emailed the picture to my illustrator and asked if the quality of the picture was good enough for the book cover. I was overjoyed when she said, "YES!"

The day that Jimmie gave the picture to me, I was stunned. I remember asking him, "How did you get this? Can I keep it?" He smiled and said, "Yes, it's yours." Over the years, the picture sat in my closet. I didn't look at it very often because it was just overwhelming to me. Today, I am so thankful that I love to look at the picture, and I see it as a precious gift that will forever be part of my life. I'm so thankful for Jimmie's sensitivity to the Lord and his proactive steps to get a copy of the picture. It's because of him that I'm able to share it with you! I never would have asked for a copy of the picture, and it's no longer hanging on the walls of the Arkansas Baptist State Convention. That is OK because the picture is in my heart, on my wall, and on the front cover of this book. Certainly, God is in the window of our lives in every way!

In the Old Testament, we see how people built altars to God so they could remember His work. This book is not an altar, but it's a time to stop, remember, and reset for the future. I give God all the praise for what He has done, is doing, and will continue to do. I trust there will be many more books in my future. I have come to accept and even enjoy the writing process. To me, speaking and writing complement one another. True Vine would be missing an important component if either the speaking or the writing side were eliminated.

When I speak, I get to develop the verbal side of my message. This is when I get to interact with people and see how the message connects with them and their lives. When I write, I get to develop the content side of my message. This is when I am forced to slow down and really think through the material God is calling me to share.

Decades ago, if you had told me, my parents, or my teachers that God would call me to write a paragraph, much less a book, we probably would have just laughed. "That's impossible! Don't set Andrea up for that type of disappointment." Thankfully, God is not in the business of doing things that make sense. Also, His plan is never disappointing. God is willing and able to do more than we can ask or imagine. My life is proof of that.

I will be forever grateful for Geyer Springs First Baptist Church and their investment in True Vine Ministry. This picture was taken during a live recording of On the Road with Ruth. The videos are available to view on my website.

CHAPTER 38

Confusing Steps and Faithful Promises

I was coasting along with True Vine Ministry. I had hit a good stride in Arkansas and was booking events and driving all over the state teaching women. I could pretty much run the ministry with my eyes closed. Life and ministry were pretty predictable. And in my experience, God doesn't prioritize safe and predictable things the way we do!

When I look back, I see how God used our finances to help us move along in the journey. When I first started True Vine, I was scared to death to speak in front of a group. However, there were bills to pay, and I needed to replace my old, steady income. As a result, I took every speaking opportunity that came my way. After ten long years, God released us from the intensely tight budget, and we were able to have some breathing room.

Then out of the blue, our budget tightened again. The boys hit the teenage years, and our bills increased. Jake played travel ball, and both boys needed new clothes and braces. Jake would be driving soon, so cars and increased insurance premiums were on the horizon. Also, saving for college was on the agenda.

Jay and I kept trying to cut costs in order to make things work. We were running out of options. We needed more income to meet the growing needs of our family. I wasn't open to going back to a normal 9-5 job. To me, that would mean True Vine was a failure.

For years, I met once or twice a year with my friend Sonny Tucker from the Arkansas Baptist State Convention. He knew the big-picture vision God had given me for True Vine and had walked that journey with me and Jay. Just as a reminder, Sonny serves as the executive director of the Arkansas Baptist State Convention (ABSC). I had often collaborated on projects or events with the ABSC but never anything permanent or long-term. Sonny and I had a meeting around the time that my family's budget was tightening, and he made a comment that I quickly dismissed. He said, "If you are ever interested in working for us, let me know."

Jay worked at a marketing firm in Conway for eighteen years and had survived numerous reorganizations and more layoffs than we cared to count. With that said, Acxiom was a great place to work, with a laid-back culture of its own. If Jay needed to leave early or work from home, he could. This was a huge asset when the boys were young and I was in seminary or traveling.

Jay had thought about making a career change several times but was never really serious about it. Finally, we knew it was time for a change. We needed more income and that was going to require us to be open to new opportunities. Jay started to make calls and sent out his resume.

Over the next few months, God blessed the plans that needed to be blessed and frustrated the plans that needed to be frustrated. Jay was aggressive with his job search and followed up on leads, but there was no progress. Months went by, and our budget got tighter and tighter. We needed to replace two vehicles, and there was some work that had to be done on our home.

We had worked hard during the ten lean years to avoid credit card debt. We always believed that one reason I was able to launch True Vine was because we had lived within our means. As a result, we were able to take a step of faith when God said, "Go!" It became obvious that I was going to need to bring in additional income for our family. I had never taken a consistent salary from True Vine. For the most part, the money stayed in the ministry and went toward ministry expenses.

Once I realized I needed to find additional income, I went into problem-solving mode. I decided I needed to find a job in Conway that didn't require mental energy. I wanted to show up, get the work done, and check it off my list. To me, this meant I could use all of my mental energy for True Vine. So many ideas went through my head during this time. I could clean houses. (One problem: I am horrible at cleaning.) I could work at Walmart or deliver newspapers or work at a bank. There were so many random ideas. One day, I remembered the comment that Sonny made to me at the ABSC. I gave him a call and asked if we could set up a time to visit.

When we had our meeting, I explained what was going on in my life. I was hoping we could find a way for me to do contract work on a regular basis. We discussed different angles and options. Sonny mentioned creating a new position in the area of women's ministry. The position would be on the Evangelism and Church Health Team. I was apprehensive about the idea. I didn't know if I could carry the vision for True Vine as well as a new position at the ABSC. I had lots of concerns, and I left the meeting that day willing to pray about it but very doubtful that it would work out.

Several weeks passed, and I didn't hear from Sonny. Jay finally landed an interview with a company in Little Rock. I was hoping the interview would lead to a job offer and a great salary. Maybe I wouldn't need to go back to work after all!

Then I received an email from Sonny's ministry assistant. She wanted to set up a meeting with me and the ABSC executive team so we could continue the discussion. (My friend and mentor Jimmie was part of that group as well as Greg Addison.) Immediately, I was nervous. The leaders of the ABSC had been so good to me over the years. I didn't want to do anything to put our relationship in jeopardy. At the same time, I had to protect my calling and True Vine. I had to be careful about taking on a position that would negatively impact my ministry. I decided to accept the invitation to the meeting and be honest about my concerns.

Over the years, I have served thousands of women in Arkansas and around the world. Some of them I have met face-to-face; others I've only had contact with through email or telephone. Naturally, there are stories and faces that stand out to me for different reasons. Maybe I saw God set them free, or maybe I related to a specific struggle in their life. I have several ladies who pray for me on a regular basis. They have my cell number and text me weekly with encouragement or scriptures. The body of Christ is a beautiful thing!

Sometimes when I receive an email from a lady I have served, I am able to open it immediately and reply. Other times, I wait until I have a block of time and reply to several at once. I try my best to reply to every email I receive. As the meeting was approaching with the ABSC executive team, I began to pray. I asked God to make His will plain to me. I asked Him to speak to me through His Word. I didn't want to base my decision off our feelings or our finances. I wanted God to speak through His Word in such a clear way that I would know if my returning to work was a "go" or "no go" answer.

On the morning of the meeting, I woke up at 3:00 a.m. My eyes shot open, and my heart was beating a little fast. I remembered I had an email in my inbox from a sweet lady in south Arkansas. She had sent the email to me several weeks earlier. For some reason, I woke up panicked about not opening and responding to the email. I decided I would open the email first thing in the morning. I went back to sleep and tossed and turned until morning. Finally, 6:30 a.m. arrived. I got up, went to my computer, and found the email. My friend wrote that she was simply saying hello and was praying for me. She gave an update about her life and family. I hadn't seen her in years, but she was one of those special gals I will never forget. We share a common bond in our adoption stories.

At the end of her message, she wrote, "I don't know why, but God prompted me to send this verse to you." It was Luke 10:2: "The harvest is plentiful, but the workers are few. Ask the Lord of the harvest, therefore, to send out workers into his harvest field." I quickly replied to the message and moved on with my day.

I drove to Little Rock for my 9:00 a.m. meeting and had a few minutes to spare. I opened my Bible reading app and the verse of the day was Luke 10:2. (I know ... you can't make this stuff up!) "The harvest is plentiful, but the workers are few. Ask the Lord of the harvest, therefore, to send out workers into his harvest field." I went into my meeting and did my best to talk Sonny and the others out of hiring me. I told them I needed to pray about it, and they needed to discuss all of the concerns I had raised. I really wanted what was best for God's work in Arkansas, both for True Vine and for the ABSC.

Again, several weeks passed. By this time, Jay and I knew that the Little Rock job interview Jay had wasn't going to work out. There was another possibility for Jay on the horizon. It was early in the process, but there was a chance he might get an interview with a new technology company that was opening an office in Conway's data district. Then I received a call from the ABSC. They wanted to set up one final meeting with me. This time, the Evangelism and Church Health team leader would be included in the mix. I prayed and asked God to show me His plan. I was still anxious about accepting a position that required me to create, cast, and maintain a ministry vision outside of True Vine. I knew it would be hard to be a good wife, mother, and ABSC employee without letting True Vine suffer.

I went into the meeting asking God to speak to me through His Word. Once again, I did my best to talk the ABSC executives out of hiring me. I even had a list of names of people I thought they should pursue. There was much discussion, and I know the guys could tell I was struggling with the decision. Finally, Terry Bostic, the team leader, looked at me and said, "Andrea, this is all I know. The harvest is plentiful, and the workers are few. I've been praying, and here is what I need to know: 'Are you willing to be a worker?'" As much as I was struggling, I knew in my heart that the Lord had confirmed His will for me. He had spoken to me through His Word. I told them I needed to talk to Jay and would let them know by noon the following day.

I drove home and cried the entire way. I was thankful for the clear direction but also confused. I immediately started questioning things. "Is this the end of True Vine? Did I do something wrong, or not do something right?" (Old scripts that run through our minds are hard to break!) I called Jay, who was on a hunting trip with the boys and my brother and told him what happened. We agreed that I should accept the job.

The next day, I made the phone call to the ABSC and accepted the women's ministry specialist position at 11:59 a.m.

The following week, Jay had an interview with Metova, the new technology company. He was offered a great position. After months of tight finances and stress about the future, we both started our new job roles on December 15, 2014! It was a whirlwind of change. The first year was a big adjustment. My job role for the ABSC allowed me to work from home. I did have to travel some during the week, and I continued to travel for True Vine on the weekends.

Slowly our family found a new rhythm. We had to let go of some of our commitments in other areas of our lives. The boys stepped up and helped, which was good for them (and hard for their protective momma!).

The job role at the ABSC was confusing to me. I never saw it coming! I promise I was more surprised than anyone else in the state of Arkansas when I accepted it. I look back now, and I get it. The job role was a good fit for both sides. It helped me get out of my routine. It pushed me to dig deep in new ways. I had to trust Jesus to help me. I wasn't able to stay in my neatly created True Vine Ministry world. A life of coasting and complacency is not on God's agenda for any of us.

For the ABSC, I knew I had to approach things differently. Women's ministry would have a new and different look. God allowed me, with the help of beautiful women from across the state, to write curriculum and develop a strategic plan for women's ministry that was based on New Testament principles.

Statewide events, roundtables, leadership training, and ministry to ministers' wives were all part of the plan. My sweet friend Shari Edwards and many other leaders from across Arkansas jumped into the trenches and worked hard to take ministry to women in Arkansas to a new level. I am so thankful for each one and how we are an extended family of sisters for one another. The work has been challenging and exciting, and the outcomes have been straight from the Lord!

One of the most meaningful aspects of my work at the ABSC has been the chance to not only fill a seat at the leadership table but also to provide this opportunity to other women. I have never been one to seek a position for the sake of making a statement or proving a point. Goodness knows I was too busy running to do that! But God has allowed me to be a part of a season of change in my state as women step into their calling and use their gifts for His glory. For that, I am forever grateful and completely humbled!

One example comes to mind, and I just have to share it with you. When I was in seminary many years ago, I took an Evangelism class. (Ironically, Sonny Tucker taught the class.) One day, the class was required to attend the statewide evangelism conference. Several of my classmates (all guys) and I rode to the conference together. When we arrived, we parked and walked to the doors of church. The greeters welcomed everyone and handed each person a program—except me. All my friends looked at me and asked if I was OK. I was fine. I knew I was in a man's world and would have to learn how to navigate it. Although I wasn't too upset, I never forgot the experience. Many years later, as an employee of the ABSC, I told Sonny the story. With great passion and determination I said, "I want to host equipping and breakout sessions for women at our statewide events. I want to use my role and influence to make a place for women at the table. I want women to know that they not only belong at our leadership events but that we have planned for them and are ready to love and equip them." Without hesitation, Sonny said, "Do it!" God is so good to bring meaning and purpose to the difficult memories and moments of life.

Arkansas is home to me, and I am passionate about my state. I love the women of Arkansas and want them to love Jesus more and more. What I thought was a confusing step turned out to be a faithful promise. God gave me two joyful ways to serve the women of Arkansas: True Vine Ministry and the Arkansas Baptist State Convention!

I can testify to the fact that the harvest is plentiful, and the workers are few. God's work is important, and each of us should be in the harvest field, seeking to serve Jesus and willing to take any step—even the confusing ones—for His glory. When we do, we will experience the faithful promises of God and know what we thought was confusing was His plan all along.

I love serving the women of Arkansas. Pictured at the top are dear friends and ministry partners. Shari Edwards, Gina Franzke, and Chris Adams.

My sweet friend Amy Cordova who serves as the Women's Missions and Ministry Specialist in Oklahoma. I love this lady to the core. So blessed to partner with her in ministry.

My sweet friend Shari Edwards following Inspire 2018. I am so thankful for Shari and the way she serves the women of Arkansas. Such a gift!

CHAPTER 39

This, I Believe!

This is one of my favorite chapters in the book, and I am so excited to share it with you! Over the years, I've always thought it would be wonderful, and important, for any ministry to have a statement of belief. This is a list of go-to statements about what you as an individual or you as a ministry believe about God, the Bible, and important faith doctrines in general.

Every single time I would sit down and begin to think about writing a statement of faith for True Vine, I would get overwhelmed. I was afraid I might leave something important out. Or maybe I would add too much. As we look through the pages of the Bible, there is so much we should believe! From Genesis all the way to Revelation, the Bible is full of promises to claim and precepts for us to follow.

One day, I decided to stop overthinking the process. I decided to sit down and type out what I believe about God, about Jesus, and about the Bible. True Vine Ministry is all about the Bible and helping women to *know the truth, live the truth,* and *share the truth.* The Bible is our source for truth!

I sat down at my computer and began to type. I didn't open my Bible, use a commentary, refer to another statement of belief, or ask a friend for help. Instead, I started pouring out all of the truths God had taught me over the years, even the truths that came from experiences in my childhood.

As I typed, my heart flooded with hope, peace, and excitement! The truths that meant so much to me, the ones I held on to during hard days or on days when I really didn't know what to believe, started pouring out of me. These are the truths that shape my life and give me a solid foundation no matter what's going on inside of me or around me.

And do you know what happened? Once I started to type, I couldn't stop. It was in that moment that I realized God had planted His Word in my life. I had been so busy and caught up in life and ministry that the most incredible aspect of my ministry and personal walk with Jesus had gone unnoticed. *God had planted His Word in my heart.* As I typed, I cried tears of joy and thankfulness. This, my sweet friend, is what I believe!

God the Father. The Father is fully God. He is our Creator, Sustainer, Protector, and Provider. He always has been, and He always will be. God is outside of time and space. He does not need anyone or anything. He is independent; yet, He graciously chooses to include us in His plan. God is holy; He is set apart and spiritually pure. There is not a shadow of darkness in Him. God is faithful, merciful, just, loving, and good. He is all sufficient and all knowing. We are made in His image, and exist to bring Him glory. He alone is worthy of our praise. This, I believe!

God the Son. Jesus is fully God. He was with God in the beginning. He always has been, and He always will be. There is no part of Jesus that is less than God. Jesus came to this earth and took on flesh. He was conceived by the Holy Spirit and born of a virgin. Jesus lived a perfect, sinless life. Jesus did amazing things during His time on the earth. He healed people, loved people, and taught people. Ultimately, He came to this earth in order to die on the cross to save us from our sins. Jesus became our substitute on the cross and satisfied God's wrath against our sin. While on the cross, He took on the punishment for our sin. He paid the price of sin in full and died a cruel death. Jesus stayed in the grave for three days. But, then He rose again! Jesus overcame sin. Jesus overcame death. Jesus overcame disease. Jesus overcame dismay. After appearing to more than five hundred people, Jesus ascended to the right hand of the Father where He sits right now, praying for you and me. He will return again, at the Father's command, and will take every believer home to heaven. Jesus provides the only way for us to enter a saving relationship with God. Jesus is the way. Jesus is the truth. Jesus is the life. This, I believe!

God the Holy Spirit. The Holy Spirit is fully God. He was with God in the beginning. He always has been, and He always will be. The role of the Holy Spirit in our lives includes teaching, leading, guiding, reminding, convicting, comforting, and empowering us. At the point of salvation, the Holy Spirit lives inside of us, and we are sealed until the day of Jesus' return. This means that once we are saved, we cannot lose our salvation. The Holy Spirit is our power source. The same power that brought Jesus out of the grave lives inside every believer in Jesus Christ. God has a plan for our lives, and it is through the Spirit of God that we are empowered to fulfill God's plan. Every Christian is given a spiritual gift. This is an area of life where we have a God-given ability to step out and lead. As we live in

God's plan for our lives, spiritual fruit is produced in and through us. The fruit of the Spirit is love, joy, peace, patience, kindness, goodness, faithfulness, gentleness, and self-control. It is through the work of the Spirit that we are able to live a full, free, and abundant life. We bring glory to God (which means we point others to God) when we live empowered by the Spirit of God. This, I believe!

Trinity. The Father, the Son, and the Holy Spirit are One God who exist in three Persons. In their "oneness," they function uniquely and in perfect unity. God is our Father, Jesus is our Savior, and the Holy Spirit is our guide. Although the word Trinity is never used in the Bible, we see the concept all over the pages of Scripture. How the Trinity functions together is a mystery to me; my mind cannot fully understand the infinite ways of God. However, the mystery doesn't make the Trinity less real to me or anyone else. This, I believe!

The Bible is God's living and breathing Word. The Bible is not an ordinary book. It is God's living and active Word and the primary way God speaks to His people. The Bible is a light that helps us see what we need to do, where we need to go, and what we need to avoid. The Bible is inspired by God. The words were given to men through the work of the Holy Spirit. God preserved these words so that we can know how to live. The Bible is God's story of love and redemption, and every word in the Bible is inspired and true. As a result, we should claim every promise and follow every principle. This, I believe!

Man is sinful and without hope apart from God's redeeming work. God created man in His image. We are distinct and different from every other created being. Because of sin, when we are born, we are born spiritually dead in our sins, separated from God, and in desperate need of God's grace. Everyone has sinned. Sin is any wrong thought, action, or reaction. Sin is serious because it separates us from God. We cannot solve our sin problem with good works or good intentions. Jesus is the only way. This, I believe!

Salvation is a free gift and the only way to move from spiritual death to spiritual life. Salvation is a work of God in a person's life. A person cannot come to a saving relationship with God based on their own efforts. (We can't be good enough or try hard enough to be saved.) God draws a person to Himself through the Holy Spirit, reveals their need for a Savior, and offers the only hope of eternal life. A person has the opportunity to respond to God's grace by placing their faith in Jesus' saving work on the cross. This, I believe!

The Church is made up of God's people. The Church is not a building or an organization; it's the people of God. The universal Church is made up of every believer in Jesus Christ regardless of race or creed. The local church is made up of believers who gather together to worship, pray, study the Bible, fellowship together, serve others, and share the gospel. Jesus is the leader of the Church. The body of Christ, also known as the Church, should love, support, and encourage one another. The Church is the bride of Christ and should eagerly await His return. The Church is God's primary plan for getting the gospel message to the ends of the earth. This, I believe!

The mission of the Church is to take the gospel of Jesus Christ to every tongue, tribe, and nation. It is easy to think that the Church exists for us. When this occurs, our preferences drive our decisions as well as our values. God's Word is clear. The Church is not about us. The Church exists to glorify God and to take the gospel message to people who need to experience

His grace. We should preach this truth, embrace this truth, and live this truth out in our local churches. When we understand the purpose of the Church, a beautiful thing happens—our needs are met as we grow in knowledge and application of God's Word to our lives. We always need to be gracious with the people we serve alongside in the local church, remembering Jesus' words: "By this everyone will know that you are my disciples, if you love one another." (John 13:35) It is crucial that we love, value, respect, honor, build up, and serve one another because we are the family of God. This, I believe!

Our daily goal is to conform to the image of Jesus. Each day, believers are called to engage in the process of sanctification. Sanctification occurs when we become more like Jesus and less like this world. God's desire for us is to become more like Jesus in the way we think, act, and react. Anything that brings us into conformity or alignment with Jesus can be used in a powerful and productive way in our lives. This, I believe!

We glorify God when spiritual fruit is produced in and through our lives. We bring glory to God when we live according to the Bible. When we do, spiritual fruit is obvious to others.

To me, a great definition of spiritual fruit is any action or reaction that points others to Jesus. We cannot produce spiritual fruit without an abiding relationship with Jesus that is empowered by the Holy Spirit. The outcome of a spiritually full and free life is the opportunity to share Jesus with other people as they look at our lives and ask, "How can you have so much hope and so much peace?" The answer is, "Only Jesus." This, I believe!

We are never alone. God is our safe place. In Him, we are wanted, welcomed, safe, and secure. Because God has a plan for our lives that is good, pleasing, and perfect, we can run to Him with confidence and know that we will find help during times of trouble. When our life feels out of control, it is not. God is always directing and always positioning us for redemption and victory. A mundane, superficial, compartmentalized life is never God's plan. Jesus came and died to secure our freedom. Biblical freedom is not distance or independence from God; rather, it is desperate dependence upon God. We are loved beyond words. We are loved by a Savior Who died on the cross to save us from our sins and Who provides the only way for us to be united with God in Heaven. This, I believe!

Diversity is a beautiful thing and should be celebrated. God's heart is for all people, and when we get to heaven, it will be the most diverse place we have ever been. Scripture teaches that every tongue, tribe, and nation will be around the throne, and we will be worshipping God together. There will be no division or struggle anymore. Every culture will be represented, and it will be the most amazing sight and sound we've ever experienced. In heaven, Jesus will wipe away every tear. There will be no more death, mourning, crying, or pain. We will worship God forever in Spirit and in Truth. This, I believe!

The day that I sat down and typed out my beliefs was transformational in every way! I realized I had a strong set of go-to beliefs that shaped my life and provided a solid foundation of daily direction and hope. I don't know where I would be without these truths. Honestly, life would be hard, desperate, and empty apart from God, His Word, and His plan.

When my boys were little, we sang a song: "The wise man built his house upon the rock, and the rains came tumbling down." If you know the song, you know that the house built on the rock stood strong while the house built on the sand went splat. Life has a way of proving simple truths. A house built on Jesus, our Rock, always stands strong.

When the boys played pee wee football, the parents were in charge of working the chains. Jay signed up, but got delayed at work. I stepped up and did it with a BIG GOLD purse on my shoulder. Who says you can't be fashion forward in football?

CHAPTER 40

Boy Mom, Oh the Smells

I am a boy mom. I love being a boy mom. Raising Jake and Andrew has helped me grow in my own personal walk with the Lord, as well as in my overall development in life. Learning to let go of control, understanding what it means to love someone with all your heart, learning what it means to just experience life with people ... Jay and the boys have given me so many chances for learning new things. And sometimes the learning happens in a funny way that I wasn't expecting!

281

Life with boys is smelly! I never know what I'm going to find, whether it's in the laundry or in the bathroom or in their bedroom. When they were little, they certainly had smells, but I could more or less control the smells by changing diapers or mopping the floor. But the more the boys grow, the more I realize that the smells are just going to be a part of life.

And so are the messes. Bedrooms are disaster zones. Dishes are left around the house. Wet clothes lie on the floor until they mildew. Sports uniforms decorate their rooms. It doesn't help (or maybe it does) that they share a bathroom. Then there's always camp laundry!

Maybe I should have expected it after all the teasing from my own family, but my boys like to give me a hard time. And now that Jake is seventeen, and Andrew is fourteen, they've gotten more creative about it. Andrew has a habit of sneaking up behind me to give me a good scare. Jake can get me stirred up in a "tizzy" faster than anyone I know. Then he slaps me on the back and says, "Aww, Mom, I'm just messing with you." But they always give me a hug afterward, and I can eventually laugh about it, too.

With as busy as life can be, I love it when they're home and we get to spend time together. Some nights we sit on the back porch and talk until late into the night. God has provided a wonderful new home for us that has an awesome back porch that is great for visiting, watching television, and grilling. Not long ago, we were in our favorite spot there, hanging out. Jay had already gone to bed because he had to get up and go to work the next day. But the boys and I stayed up, talking about life, and about their plans, and how football was going to start back up soon.

I was relaxed and thinking, "We're having this beautiful moment together as a mom with her two sons ..." And then they must have communicated somehow to each other without me knowing, because they suddenly both tossed mini-firecrackers that were left over from the Fourth of July at my feet. The firecrackers went off at the same time, and I jumped and screamed. I may have woken the neighbors up! That's just one example of what it's like to live life with boys.

We have been through so many seasons as a family: the baby years when there was sleep deprivation, the toddler years when there were tantrums, the elementary school years when there were fights. In the preteen years, they had to be driven all over the place, and then back again, with me as a taxi driver—the hamster-wheel life! I've always tried to enjoy and celebrate each season for what it represents: new growing and learning chances for all of us.

And now we're coming into a new phase of life where they're much more independent and able to care for themselves. They wake themselves up in the morning, make their own lunches, take care of their homework. Jake drives himself wherever he needs to go, and Andrew will soon be doing the same thing. Soon we will be launching these boys out of our house and into the independent years, whether that's college or work or marriage, or some combination. Whatever life has in store for them. I've tried to look for the positives in each season and not be too sad when it's time to transition.

One transition that I struggled with more than any of the others was when Jake started to drive. Jake had been my little boy; I always saw him as needing me. And the first time he got in the car and drove out of the driveway, I had a panic attack. I was short of breath, my heart started beating fast, and my palms were clammy. It seemed so wrong. There was no way I could make sure Jake was going where he was supposed to be going or doing what he was supposed to be doing. (Hello, control issues!)

I didn't want to text him to find out if he was OK. If I texted him, he might take his eyes off the road. I didn't want to call him, because what if he had to look down to answer his phone and drove off the road? I was at a loss for what to do in that moment. Not that Jake wanted or needed any help; he had a lot of experience and had become a good driver. I just wanted to be there for him!

I knew he had a couple of friends with him, so I called one of them. I calmed down a little when they picked the phone up and answered calmly. "Hello?" "Noah, I just need to be on the phone with all of you while Jake is driving you around town. Where are you guys right now?" It turned out that they were on the interstate, going 75 miles an hour at the time. Imagine the panic of a mom who finds out her son and his friends are on the interstate for the first time together at that speed ... and there's nothing she can do about it!

"Noah, is Jake a good driver?"
"Yes, ma'am, he is," came the reply.
"Does he have both hands on the wheel?"
"Yes, ma'am, he does." I breathed a little easier but not much.
"Is everyone buckled up?"
"Yes, ma'am, everyone is buckled up."

"Where are you going to next?"

"We're taking Perry home."

That brought all the panic back, because I knew they had to drive by a lake that I think is extremely dangerous because there's no guardrail. So I talked them through how it's important, when you're going around the corner, to slow down and keep both hands on the wheel and to make sure you're focusing and that nobody's talking so Jake could take the corner safely. (The irony of it all is that I was the one who needed to stop talking!)

The next thirty minutes seemed like an eternity as I paced around the house, praying and claiming every Scripture I could remember! "Lord, all the days written for him were ordained before even one of them came to be!" "Lord, lead him (to drive) on level ground!" I was a sight to see. The good news is that Jake dropped his friends off safely and then came home safely himself. I will admit that it took several months until I could relax whenever Jake went for a drive.

I thrive on heart-to-heart conversations where we can talk about our feelings and thoughts. When I'm the one driving the car, the boys have no way to escape these conversations! Often, I ask Jake and Andrew for a 1-10 rating on how they're doing. One means "I'm doing horrible," while ten means "I'm doing great." They may roll their eyes at my questions, but they never complain when we drive to Sonic for something to drink.

Jake recently turned seventeen, and he continues to be a strong leader who is determined and passionate about the things and people that matter to him. He's loyal and always takes care of his friends. Jake has strong principles, and he lives by them. You always know where you stand with Jake, and it has been a joy to watch him take the lead at school, church, and at work. Recently, our church cooked a big breakfast for all the football players on the morning of a big game. Even though Jake is a football player and could've gotten out of helping with the breakfast, he was glad to show up at church the night before and help cook. Before long, Jake was organizing the kitchen and making sure I didn't burn the eggs!

One thing I have to tell you about Jake is the incredible way he understood the purpose of True Vine from a very young age. He "got" what I was called to do and always pushed me to reach more people and to write more books and to step out in new ways. God has used Jake to challenge me in my vision for the ministry. For the longest time, I told people, "I don't need an agent. I have Jake."

Andrew is happy being Andrew. He loves his easygoing life that is full of friends and family. When he comes home from school, he checks on Lulu, grabs a snack, jumps on his bike, and heads out in the neighborhood to find some friends. He loves to be outside. Fishing, camping, and hiking are always on the top of his weekend plans.

Andrew helps our family slow down and enjoy life. He has a great sense of humor and can catch me off guard by playing practical jokes. He has a confidence within him that I admire. He knows who he is and thrives in his own skin. I love that about Andrew! He's loyal and strongly committed to our church and his youth group. If the doors are open at church, he wants to be there. Andrew serves others without complaining. He recently found out that I was asked to be in a dunking booth for a citywide outreach event hosted by our church. The moment Andrew realized I was anxious about being in the booth, he volunteered to take my spot.

One year I was at a parent-teacher conference for Andrew. His teacher bragged on Andrew to me. "He's thoughtful and compassionate, he's willing to help others when they need something, and he has a great sense of humor. He's a leader in his own way, and the kids in the class really like him." Then she smiled and said, "I want a copy of your book!"

She meant, "However you parent him, I want to know how you've done that." Of course, I took her literally, and said, "Oh! OK, well, how many copies do you want?" It was so embarrassing once I figured out what she really meant. She had no idea I had actually written any books. I told Andrew the story when I got home, and he was embarrassed about it. I laughed and laughed!

I am forever grateful and completely in love with the most influential person in Jake and Andrew's lives ... their dad! Jay is an awesome husband and father. He leads and serves our family so well. Jay is an involved dad who sits at the kitchen table and helps with homework, attends all the ball games, and provides rock-solid guidance. He is patient and brings stability to our family. He has poured so much time, love, and energy into all of us, and we are better for it! Jay is a visible leader at church. He serves as a deacon, small-group leader, mission-team leader, and helps with the youth. I know

Jake and Andrew watch their dad and learn what it means to be a man of honor and character.

Both of my kids have always really liked going to church. Church has been a big part of our family life, and it has been a non-negotiable. But at the same time, it has never been a struggle or a battle. It's who we are as a family, and it's what we do. We structure our family calendar around our local church calendar, and for my kids, that's the norm. They haven't fought it, and I thank God for that. They're not only involved in their youth group but in K-LIFE as well. K-LIFE is a discipleship program in our city.

When I first became a mom, I took on the role of project manager. I was going to shape and mold, direct and control. I think the transition from when I started my parenting journey until now is that I have moved from seeing them as projects to embracing them as blessings. I am their mom. I want to encourage and bless them. I want to correct and teach them. I want to be present and involved in their lives. My family—that's the real deal for me.

At the end of the day, they're my legacy, not my projects. They're my first and foremost ministry, and they are the best gifts God has given to me and Jay. The transition from project manager to mom has changed my world. It has melted my heart to embrace them for who they are and for the plans God has for them and to just know that I get to be a part of that. I'm forever grateful.

Sports, food, and washing uniforms. All part of raising boys! #boymom

In the locker room following a Conway High School Wampus Cat win!

Part of my Mom Tribe! Jenifer, Sonya and I were celebrating an overtime victory in Russellville, Arkansas. (Jenifer Kendrick is next to me and Sonya Williams is behind me.)

A mom and her boys! I love cheering for these two in sports and in life.

The boys love to hunt with Uncle Jason. This was a good day with lots of ducks.

This picture was taken on the first day Jake drove and I sat in the passenger seat. Talk about hard! My taxi cab days were coming to an end!

CHAPTER 41

Balancing Life and Family

Disclaimer: This chapter is gut-level honest. Proceed with caution!

Just like any family, we have our share of struggles. Jay and I are constantly trying to strike a balance between life, family, and ministry. We juggle spending time together, spending time with our kids, spending time with friends, checking on our extended family, and doing what we feel called to do at church, in our community, and around the world. Then we have our jobs and True Vine, too. Sometimes it's just a lot as we try to figure out how the puzzle pieces fit together for a healthy life and family. We have to navigate all of these commitments and roles on a daily, weekly, and monthly basis.

There are seasons that are really busy between my speaking engagements, the kids' schedules, and Jay's work. We usually thrive during most of these seasons, but toward the end, we all get tired and grumpy and start going through the motions. We can tell when our attitudes are starting to slip. Our patience is shorter, and we start putting our own needs before each other's needs. These are sure signs that we have overextended ourselves. I'm easily overwhelmed during these times and any little mishap can cause me to want to quit everything. I will start to talk about all of my roles and how busy I am and how I can't do it all, and then it turns into a full-on whining session and a declaration that I am stepping back from everything! (Another sign of overextending!)

One thing that we have to work on is communication. Sometimes we get so busy that we find ourselves simply sharing facts with each other instead of really connecting and communicating. "What meetings do you have this week?" "What is your travel schedule next week?" "What ballgames are on the calendar?" "What do I need to pick up at the store?" When we are busy, we focus on the facts—just the facts.

Technology is another area that can be hard. Technology provides a way for us to be in our own worlds in a negative way, so that even if we're in the same room together, we're really not communicating with one another or present in the moment. All four of us have phones, and we spend lots of time on them. The kids play games or watch videos, I am on social media or texting, and Jay is checking his emails. This can happen way too often if we are not careful. And, for the kids, it seems normal because everyone they know has and uses phones nonstop.

Another struggle that we face as the kids get older is protecting our family time. Sometimes it's easier to let the kids do things with their friends instead of the four of us really trying to create a moment where we're all connecting. We easily fall into the trap of "microwaving" family time, checking that off our list, and then getting back to our busy schedules. Being disciplined during the busy seasons and saying to the kids, "You know what? We haven't had any family time, so we're going to do something—just the four of us," isn't always our first response. I think we easily give our family time away instead of carving out what we need to do as a family, telling the boys, and then letting them supplement that with friend time.

At the same time, the boys are at the age where there is less family time and more friend, school, work, and church time. I try to think about the boys and their stage of life and figure out what is the best for every member of our family. One good thing that is happening as the boys get older is that there is more time for me and Jay to go on lunch dates and day trips!

The best thing I started to do to help balance life, family, and ministry was taking the summers off from True Vine speaking engagements. I made that decision several years ago and have stuck to it. Our family goes hard from mid-January to the second week of May. The summers are purposefully slow and easy. I am home most of the time. Pool days, friend outings, vacations, catching up on writing, and big cups of coffee are on the agenda.

I try to do more devotional writing and reading as opposed to deep research. I ask the Lord to fill my cup, and He always does. I can't tell you the difference this makes in my life. Once mid-August hits and the kids are back in school, we put the pedal to the metal until the second week of November. The boys play football, so we can have up to three games per week. Jay and I try to make it to every game, but if we can't, we find a practice during the week to watch. This yearly schedule has created a rhythm in our lives that works. It's not always perfect, but it is our game plan for life, family, and ministry.

It's inevitable that our life, family, and ministry worlds collide. I remember booking a weekend retreat in Kentucky without checking the school calendar. I booked the event one year ahead of time, so it never crossed my mind that it might be homecoming weekend. Once I realized the conflict, it was too late. The day before I boarded the plane for Kentucky, I made sure all the clothes, corsages, and food for the after party were staged at the right houses. I did everything I could to make the night go as smoothly as possible. I boarded my flight early the next morning but was delayed in Dallas due to bad weather. I ran from concourse to concourse trying to find a flight that would get me to Kentucky in time to speak that night. I cried and prayed for a flight. All the while, I was texting Jay to make sure he was getting everyone where they needed to be. I finally made it to Kentucky and literally walked in the door of the church as I was being introduced, one hour after the event started. Later that night, I made it to the hotel and settled in for the night. I texted with my amazing mom-friends until 2:00 a.m. They wanted me to feel like I was there with them enjoying all the homecoming activities.

I have to give a shout-out to my mom tribe because I wouldn't be able to serve in ministry without them. Jenifer Kendrick, Lacie Thomas, Kyla Garrett, and so many others have been consistently there for our family over the years. I remember one conversation with Jenifer that still brings tears to my eyes. We carpooled together for years. Jen always covered extra carpool duty because of my travel schedule. I felt so bad about that and always wanted to make it up to her. I remember her saying, "Andrea this is my part in your ministry. This is what I can do to help the women you are serving." I was so blessed by that. One day Jenifer went with me to a speaking engagement at her home church in Nashville, Arkansas. She introduced me that night and told the crowd, "Between the two of us, we make one really good mom." So true!

One time Jay was the culprit of home life colliding with my speaking engagements. On that trip, I had been invited to speak to the student body at Williams Baptist University in northeast Arkansas. I arrived on campus the night before and met with some of the young women to share about my life and ministry. The college reserved a room for me on campus, and I checked in and set my alarm for the next morning. I woke up and did what I always do. I took a shower and washed my hair. I have unusually oily hair, so I wash it every single day. When I used the shampoo that I brought, I noticed that the consistency was a little odd. When I rubbed it into my hair and tried to work it into a lather, I realized something was very wrong.

I looked at the bottle, and it was labeled "shampoo," but what was in that bottle was clearly not shampoo. Apparently, my husband had taken an old shampoo bottle and put homemade shaving cream in it. The shaving cream happened to be made out of pure coconut oil. Then without even thinking, Jay put the bottle of "shampoo" in my travel drawer with all the other travel-size soaps and lotions.

The oil would not come out, no matter how much I rinsed it. It was a disaster. I got out of the shower and dried my hair, but it still looked wet. I walked to the front desk acting like everything was normal and asked if there was a place on campus to buy shampoo. The young lady working the front desk was so sweet and really tried not to react to the state of my hair. She told me there was not a place on campus to buy shampoo. I went back to my room and did my best to get the oil out of my hair by using conditioner. I can't even describe the situation in words. My hair felt like it weighed ten pounds.

I made it to the chapel and put on my headset microphone. I stood in front of the entire student body with the greasiest hair you have ever seen. I did notice that when I took my headset off, it had a nice, oily residue on it. When I got home, Jay took one look at me and asked, "What happened to you?" "You did!" I replied, with a smile. We now have strict rules about labeling bottles that are filled with "homemade" concoctions. We have laughed and laughed about this story more times than I can count.

Balancing life and ministry is an ongoing process for us. It's one of the hardest aspects of our family's life. We have good seasons and bad seasons. Through it all, we try to admit when we make mistakes, regroup, and try harder the next time. Life is a journey for all of us. One thing is certain: Jay and I don't want to look back and have regrets when it comes to our family. We really want to get it right.

Jay and I have been married for 22 years and counting! I love this man!

Jake and Andrew are brothers to the core. Love these two!

CHAPTER 42

Spiritual Legacy

Just like when we were young, I remain close to my siblings Jason and Shannon. We're very involved in each other's lives. When we were younger, we spent a lot of time together because we were so close in age. We rode bikes, we fought, we went on trips, we jumped on the trampoline, we swam in the pool, we made lots of memories. And now it's so fun to see our children doing the same things with one another.

Jason has two children, and Shannon has three. Our mom and dad love spending time with their kids and grandkids. All of us spend a lot of time together on the holidays. We take family vacations together. We try to see each other as often as possible. We're very involved in each other's lives to this day, and I am so grateful for that. My parents come to our house often; they have a room and a bathroom ready for them anytime they want to spend the night.

My friends and family all like to give me a hard time, which is hilarious for everyone. I am often the butt of the jokes; I have that blonde personality, and I fall for it every single time.

Every Christmas, my family does a "white elephant" gift exchange. Everybody brings one gift, and we put the wrapped gifts in the center of the table and draw numbers. Then we have a chance to either pick a gift from the table or steal a gift from somebody who has already opened one. You never know what you're going to get, and you always try to bring a gift that people will fight over. My approach has always been the same. I bring a gift to the exchange that is something I want and then I always try to bring my gift home with me.

My family has figured this out, and they all work together to make sure that anything can happen, as long as I don't get the gift I want. Now it's become this game where it's everybody against me. It's super funny. My dad leads the charge. He's the kindest man, he's a genuine man, and he's a man of wisdom and character. But when it comes to Christmastime, he has one goal, and that is to make sure I don't get the gift I want because I throw an all-out fit every single time. I know I'm doing it, and I try not to, but it's just so much fun, and we laugh so hard whenever we're playing this game.

One year, my brother had purchased a fake lottery ticket, and he knew it would be so funny if he could figure out a way for me to open the lottery ticket, scratch off the numbers, and believe I had won. He came up with a plan and everyone was in on the plan. He knew I would never play the lottery and would have a few words of wisdom to share about playing the lottery. Something like, "You know there are better ways to spend your money," or "That's not really honoring to the Lord, and we don't want to do anything that isn't honoring to the Lord." He knows me well.

It was my turn to pick a gift in the white elephant gift exchange. Somehow, and I still to this day don't know how it happened, I ended up opening a box that contained fuzzy socks, some lotion, and a lottery ticket. I saw the warm, fuzzy socks and got super excited about them. I like fuzzy socks! Then I saw the lotion, and it smelled so good. Then I looked at the lottery ticket, and it was almost like a crisis of faith. It was as if my family was leading a lamb to the slaughter. They were all in on it but were playing it super cool.

My first response was, "Oh, I'm not going to scratch it off. I don't play the lottery. Somebody else can have this ticket." But Jason slowly coaxed me into it. "There's nothing wrong with it, Andrea. We're just here among family. No one is going to know you played the lottery. We won't post it on social media. Here, I've got a penny.

How about you just scratch off a couple of the numbers and see what happens? It's not like it's going to be a winner, anyway. There are only a few winning tickets. Just do it."

"Well, I guess I could just scratch off a few ... ." I took the penny and scratched off the first number. Since it was a fake ticket, it didn't matter what I scratched off—it was going to be a winner. Then, I scratched off the second one and saw that it was a match. I started to get a little excited inside, thinking, "Well, what if I do have a winning ticket?" Then I started to have another crisis. "What will I do if I win? Will I tell anybody or not? Will I turn it in? Will I claim the money? What could I do with the money? Maybe I could give it to the church and do something good with it. Maybe I could use it for the ministry; I've been needing a new computer and some new signage ... Maybe this is God's provision!"

I was gone—hook, line, and sinker. So, I scratched off the third number, and realized I had a winning ticket. I had just won $10,000. I started squealing with excitement. "Can y'all believe it? I have $10,000!" About one minute into it, I realized I was being recorded, and everyone was laughing at me. It was a joke, and I had totally fallen for it. That is a great picture of life with my extended family. It is fun, it is full, it is meaningful. And it is very unpredictable! I'm so thankful for that.

Another thing that has become a tradition is that Jason, Jay, Jake, and Andrew hunt together. They have an annual hunting trip that they take together over Thanksgiving break, and they hunt deer and duck. The stories that they come home telling are pretty wild. My brother is just as fun and unpredictable as he was when we were growing up. He loves to tell my boys stories about me and how he used to give me a hard time. When I was in junior high, he would threaten to put me in the trash can at school, to the point where I would break down in tears. He'll tell them childhood stories, and my boys love that. What I love is seeing the faithfulness of God and how he has brought my family together to where we really have an extended group of people who are rock solid for each other. I know that both my brother and my sister would do anything to help me, and I would do anything to help them.

Recently Jason, Shannon, and I hosted a reception to celebrate our parents' fiftieth wedding anniversary. We all gathered together in Paris, Arkansas, where we grew up. At the end of the reception, Jason, Shannon, and I stood up and blessed our parents. We talked about how my dad is a man of wisdom, loyalty, and character and how if there's anything we need, he goes above and beyond to make sure he provides that for us. We talked about my mom, and how she is a person of strength and grace, and how she is wise in her understanding of how to love and serve us in our different seasons of life. We love our parents so much, and we wouldn't pick anyone else!

We have a lot of fun as a family, but there is a spiritual depth and legacy that is important to understand. My parents valued church and their relationship with

Christ. They put us in the places where we would be exposed to grace and receive it as God faithfully drew us to Himself. For years, I attributed the yearning in my heart to serve God and His people to the hard spot of loneliness and isolation that I experienced as a child. Without a doubt, it was a contributing factor because whenever I went into the church, those feelings went away. Even when I was running from God, there was this place within me that wanted God and needed Him desperately. I think what I am just now realizing is that the spiritual hunger was also fueled by the spiritual heritage built into my life by my parents. This is a heritage I want to pass down to my children.

Jay's family is also a big part of our lives. Jay's mom, Cindy, has battled cancer for several years and does so with an incredible amount of faith. Jay's dad, Joe, is an incredible caregiver and the most selfless man we know. Joe and Cindy have been passionate about taking the gospel of Jesus to the nations for many years. They went on many overseas mission trips prior to cancer changing the direction of their lives. Their hearts have been with the people of Africa, and they will always be deeply invested in reaching that people group with the hope of Jesus.

Growing up, Jay and his brother Blake watched Joe and Cindy live out their faith. Joe and Cindy were serious about Bible study, they were serious about mission work, and even though Jay ran from all of that for a while, he had been exposed to it his entire life. Jay received Christ when he was eight years old and grew up going to church.

After Cindy was diagnosed with cancer, and life became a series of trips to the hospital for therapy, Joe and Cindy found new ways to live on mission for Jesus. Serving in their local church, befriending homeless people, ministering to those in jail, and serving on an Indian reservation not far from their home in northwest Arkansas became the new way to share the love of Jesus with others. Jay definitely attributes his spiritual foundation to his parents and grandparents.

Joe and Cindy recently celebrated the fiftieth wedding mark. While it was a cold and rainy day outside, the love and warmth in the room was a great testimony to their lives. They love Jesus, and they love people! We have so much to be thankful for with this milestone given that Cindy's battle with cancer has been intense over the years. God has sustained her life, and we are thankful for the many wonderful memories and look forward to making many more!

A lasting legacy of family and faith has been given to Jay and me. What blesses me more than anything is to know that while Jay and I were running from God, He was orchestrating all the events of our lives. We were running, and He was protecting and guiding. When we returned to the Lord and started living on mission, I know there were so many factors involved. Our family heritage was a huge part of that. Our parents had loved us and raised us to love Jesus. They had poured into our lives, and God used their influence to shape us.

Jay and I want to provide the same legacy for Jake and Andrew. Although it has been a journey, we've tried to give up control and live with a heart of surrender, saying, "Lord, wherever You tell us to go, we will go. Whatever You tell us to do, we will do it." As time goes on, I can see the passing down of spiritual heritage from generation to generation to generation.

This past summer, both boys went on mission trips, and it was so rewarding to see them carry on the legacy of taking the gospel to others. Our boys were called, and they responded to the call. Andrew went to Florida with our church, and he worked so hard there. I loved hearing the reports of how he shared, led, and served. Jay and Jake went to the other side of the world and helped host a medical clinic in Southern Europe. At the end of the clinic, the gospel was shared with every single person who came through. Jay and Jake were able to do that together.

I'm excited about the next generation of missionaries who will come through our family, and I give God all the glory for that. I realize the call on their lives and the way they will respond to the call will be different. Jay and I want the boys to find their place in life and ministry and have the best time doing it. Like us, they will make their share of mistakes, and there will be lessons to learn. Our family is a place where perfection is not the goal. We just want to be real—the good, the bad, and the ugly. It's all part of the journey.

You never know how God is going to redeem the broken and wasted years, but He is faithful to redeem every single one of them. Everyone leaves a legacy. We all make our mark. I am excited about my life, family, and ministry carrying on a spiritual legacy that outlives me and my short time on this earth.

James and Sandra Morris celebrating fifty years of marriage! I love my parents so much.

Joe and Cindy Lennon celebrating fifty years of marriage! Their lives are a true reflection of God's love. I love them very much.

The Lennon family at Joe and Cindy's house in Rogers, Arkansas.

CHAPTER 43

Looking Ahead

God in His great wisdom allows His plans and purposes to unfold little by little. This is a truth that we need to understand and accept. We don't have a road map. We don't know all of the stops, twists, and turns that lie ahead. For those of us who like to be in control, this can be a difficult truth to accept. At the same time, it paves the way for an exciting, God-size journey.

When I was a teenage girl, I went through *Experiencing God*, a Bible study by Dr. Henry Blackaby. *Experiencing God* focuses on developing a passionate love relationship with Jesus. One principle stood out to me. It was the idea that we need to see where God is at work and join

Him there. These days, when I think of that principle, I look back at my life and laugh. My tendency has been to see where God is at work, and then do my best to run away or talk Him and others out of it.

Today I am at a different place. I don't want to run from God's work, and I don't want to talk Him or others out of it. So, as I think about what is ahead, there are a few areas where God seems to be doing something. I don't know the outcome of any of the areas, but I'm looking for ways to join Him. (Hello, progress for me!)

Radio: Christian radio is a staple in my life. I listen to it every time I am in the car. A few years ago, I spoke at an event in the central Arkansas area. Little did I know that Steve Marston's wife was in the audience. Steve is a well-known Christian radio host in Arkansas, working for Salem Media. Following the event, Steve's wife went home and told Steve about True Vine Ministry.

One day I was sitting in the parking deck at the University of Arkansas for Medical Sciences just before heading into the hospital to visit Jay's mom who was battling cancer. Then my phone rang and I heard a very familiar voice—a voice I had heard many times on the radio. It was Steve, and he invited me to come to Little Rock and visit the station of Faith Talk Radio. He was honest about his reason for calling. He said, "We want to explore a partnership with True Vine. We would like for you to host a weekly radio program." I just about died. I never saw that opportunity coming. I did my typical Andrea routine: "I'll pray about that."

After several contacts from Steve and others, I finally agreed to visit the station. I met all of the great folks and was asked to record a guest spot. I agreed. We recorded an eight- to ten-minute interview, and I left thinking, "I'm glad that is behind me."

Over the next few years, Salem Media folks continually reached out to me and kept the lines of communication open. They invited me to be a part of their events, and I finally started to really pursue this opportunity. I was so nervous about a weekly show, but it was obvious God was opening the door, and I needed to walk through it. I agreed to host the show, and my home church stepped up once again and provided the funds to make it happen. (Oh, how I love the work of God through the local church!) *Truth on the Go with Andrea Lennon* recently hit the airwaves! You can listen to the podcast of the programs on my website.

International Work: As the saying goes, hindsight is 20-20. I think this is true in every area of life, including ministry. I know God has a plan for me in the area of international work. I don't know all the details, but I can look back and see how God has been doing a specific work in this area of my life. He is calling me to think beyond Arkansas and the United States.

I told you about the way God connected me with an editor when I wrote *Reflecting His Glory*. What I didn't tell you about was the neat thing I learned in the process. The editor happened to be a lady who lived and served overseas. Initially, I didn't see the significance of this connection. Once I did, I never turned back. She taught me the importance of having an international perspective.

I was born and raised in the South, in the Bible Belt no less. It's easy for me to communicate using terms that relate to "my people" right here in the USA. I was so thankful for an editor who challenged me to move beyond this narrow vision. She held my feet to the fire (there is another southern phrase!) and helped me to see that the world we live in is BIG and that everyone needs to know about Jesus and understand His teachings.

As I wrote with an international perspective, I learned how to be purposeful and strategic when it comes to reaching the lost world. On each of my book projects, I have used some form of international help. Typically, this comes in the form of an editor or a writing coach who lives and serves Jesus overseas. The insights that they bring to the table are invaluable.

I love a full-circle moment. A full-circle moment occurred for me on Hollywood Boulevard in Los Angeles. Jay and I were in California to explore mission opportunities as well as share the love of Jesus on international television. (I shared this story with you in chapter 32.)

The day after we recorded the live broadcast, our friend Ara took us sightseeing. We walked up and down Hollywood Boulevard and stopped at a coffee shop along the way. We ordered something to drink and sat outside and watched as hundreds of people walked by. The people passing by were of every race and ethnicity; no two people looked the same.

Ara looked at me and said, "I want to help you with your ministry. We need more women Bible teachers whose materials can be translated into other languages. I have the international connections. I can help make it happen." For years, my ministry vision had been narrow and, quite honestly, "Americanized." As I sat and soaked in the moment, for the first time, I wasn't afraid. I was sure that if God opened that door, I needed to walk through it. God had prepared the way by connecting me with international writers who helped get the message ready for an international audience. I never would have thought beyond Arkansas on my own. My vision for True Vine Ministry had always been based on staying in the safe and comfortable places. I was not well traveled or even aware of God's work all over the world. The nations were not on my radar screen. Looking back, I knew that the nations were on God's radar screen for me. I was certain of it.

Since that day, God has continued to open international doors for me. I am connecting with more and more people each year who are serving all over the world. In many ways, I'm still waiting and watching to see how the international work is going to happen. I know it's not a matter of "if" but "when." At the same time, I know it's already happening. God is doing a work that I'm not even fully aware of, and I love that!

I love to tell my adoption story. What a blessing to share it with the readers of Encourage Magazine in the Fall of 2017.

My sweet hubby and I at the Faulkner Lifestyle Magazine launch party in April of 2018.

Truth on the Go with Andrea Lennon hit the airwaves in December of 2017. I am pictured in the studio of 93.3 The Fish and 99.5 Faith Talk Radio with my sweet friend and producer Bethany.

CHAPTER 44

Letting Go of Control

Not long ago, I had the chance to meet Dr. Henry Blackaby and his precious wife. Decades after I first went through his book, *Experiencing God*, Dr. Blackaby is now in his eighties. One thing is certain: His love for Jesus and the church is still strong.

I shared with Dr. Blackaby the way God used his *Experiencing God* Bible study to help shape my view of life. I told him how the principle of "seeing where God is at work and joining him" had challenged me over the past twenty-five years. I remember that more than anything I wanted to thank him and make sure he knew that his work was still impacting lives—especially mine!

After I finished talking, Dr. Blackaby leaned back on the pew where he was seated, closed his eyes, and shared the following thoughts with me. I wish I could remember the exact words he said, but the heart of it has stayed with me. He told me that God doesn't need us, but He graciously chooses to use us. Great things happen when we make ourselves available to Him. I listened to Dr. Blackaby's words and quietly prayed that God would make them a reality in my life.

I started this book by confessing that the pull to live by faith and the pull to be in control have been constant companions to me. I want to end this book by saying, letting go of control and enjoying the spacious land of faith is slowly becoming my new reality.

God consistently has taught me to value the beautiful act of surrender. To be honest, I can't believe I didn't jump on board with surrender many years ago. Our God is the faithful God Who has incredible plans for us. Why would we follow or trust anyone else? Relationships, experiences, opportunities—even ourselves—all fall short of providing real hope, meaning, and direction. God, on the other hand, never falls short. He is the One Who sees all things, knows all things, controls all things, and ultimately provides direction for our lives.

Letting go of control is hard because we have to place our trust in God and His plan. Each morning when I wake up, I greet the day with the following thought: "Lord, today, You are the Leader, and I am the follower. You are the Savior, and I am the sinner. You are the Vine, and I am the branch.

You are the Potter, and I am the clay. You are the Shepherd, and I am the sheep. You are the Creator, and I am the creation." As I do this, I am reminded of Who God is and how He faithfully works in and through our lives.

"This is what the Lord says, he who made the earth, the Lord who formed it and established it—the Lord is his name: 'Call to me and I will answer you and tell you great and unsearchable things you do not know.'" (Jeremiah 33:2-3)

What an incredible offer God extends to us each day. He offers to lead our lives and tell us things we don't know. As I call on Him, His unsearchable riches of love, knowledge, wisdom, and grace are made available to me. Oh, yes, letting go of control is a great place to be! We are at our best when we recognize that God created us and knows what is best for us in every situation we face. Embracing this truth positions our hearts to hear from God in a way that is open to respond with a "Yes!" no matter the call He places on our lives.

So, what do I want to do with the rest of my life? I'm so glad you asked! I want to make myself available to God. I believe that in God's economy, a surrendered life has so much potential! I want His will, His way, and His power to work in and through my life. I hope I never measure spiritual success based on the number of followers I have, the books I've written, the places I've traveled, or the people I've met.

I want to measure spiritual success based on three things: trusting God, surrendering to His plan, and following Him in simple obedience. Nothing more and nothing less. I believe that the outcome to this type of life is incredible. I believe that it will bring peace as I rest in the power of God's loving and all-sufficient hand.

I think about the day I was born and how God was in complete control. A helpless baby, in the nursery of a hospital, waiting on a family. Yet, not one aspect of my life was "up in the air." I am thankful for the journey to a place of peace. Peace with God. Peace with myself. Peace with others. Peace with His plan.

I don't know the details of your journey. Maybe, like me, you have experienced some struggles. The struggles keep us real and desperate for Jesus. Here is some good news: We don't have to stay in that hard, tight spot that leaves us empty, questioning, or unable to breathe. Jesus came to bring freedom to that spot, and He is willing and able to bring abundant healing through that spot.

How do we experience freedom? Scripture says, "Where the Spirit of the Lord is, there is freedom." (2 Corinthians 3:17) Invite Jesus to invade that hard spot and heal it with His power and love. The moment you do, you are opening up your life to experience all of His goodness and grace.

I find myself constantly praying, "Lord, I want all of You in all of me, and all of me living for all of You!" I don't want to have any off-limit areas. *I simply want God to be in control of my life.*

Through writing this book, it has been so clear to me that at every crossroad, I ran from my calling. When opportunities were presented to me, I did my best to explain them away or convince myself or others I wasn't ready or able. Probably one of the biggest blessings of writing *God in the Window* has been the realization that I have been running from my calling—even while I have been trying to fulfill it. Here's the deal: That stops today. Instead of running from my calling, I'm going to start running toward my calling. Imagine the difference that type of running will make in my life!

I'm going to stop playing it safe and keeping things under wraps. I'm going to run to the opportunities and embrace them and trust God to do what only He can do. This book has been integral in my decision to let go of control. I have a certainty and a confidence in my heart that I'm exactly where I am supposed to be in my life and ministry. I think revisiting our stories has a way of clarifying where we are and where God is calling us to go. I am thankful for that!

God has the power to redeem, change, and transform our lives. I'm an example of God setting His child free! Whenever I think about His work in my life, I get so excited and so overwhelmed, because if He can change me, He can change anyone. I'm so passionate about the Lord and His Word. Think about how many times the Lord met me through His Word and directed or corrected me. God is so good to challenge us. He is so faithful to lead us every single step of the way. It's exciting to know that each morning we can wake up and ask God to rule and reign over our day. What an opportunity we have to submit to Him and for Him to lead us!

God is in the window of our lives. I am certain of it! He sees us, knows us, loves us, and offers a life that is beyond our wildest dreams. Let's decide together—right now—not to settle for less than His best.

The Lennon Family

Connect With Andrea!

Come see what True Vine is all about.
www.andrealennonministry.org

EPILOGUE

The Beauty of Adoption

One of my favorite things about my story is that I am adopted. Adoption shows what Jesus did for us by providing the only way for us to be welcomed into the family of God. The Bible explains clearly that, because of sin, we are born spiritually dead and separated from God. We are without a spiritual family. Our sin problem is huge. It is so huge, we cannot do anything to solve it. We are helpless and in desperate need of grace.

When I was in the hospital nursery, I was also helpless and in need of grace. I didn't have the ability to save myself. I needed the undeserved favor of a family—a family who would bring me into their home and make me their child. I couldn't make myself a member of their family. My parents had to initiate the relationship and provide the way.

The same is true in our spiritual lives. Before we were born, God stepped into our sin dilemma and provided the only way for us to be saved. Jesus, the perfect Son of God, came to this earth, lived a perfect life, and died in our place. He showed us the true meaning of love and grace.

- Romans 3:23 says, "For all have sinned and fall short of the glory of God." That is right: We all have sin in our lives, and we can't do anything to solve our sin problem.

- Our sin is serious because it separates us from God. Romans 6:23 says, "For the wages of sin is death, but the gift of God is eternal life in Christ Jesus our Lord." Thankfully, Jesus is the answer to our sin problem!

- Romans 10:9 says, "If you declare with your mouth, 'Jesus is Lord,' and believe in your heart that God raised him from the dead, you will be saved."

You can receive the love and grace of God by confessing your sin to Him, asking Jesus to forgive you for your sin, and trusting that Jesus' death on the cross and resurrection from the grave paid the price for your sin.

Right now, stop and talk to Jesus. Tell Him about your sin and your need to be saved from it. Cry out to Him and ask Him to save you. He will! He loves you and has an amazing plan for your life. You are wanted! You are welcomed! You can be free from the weight of your sin and struggle!

There is something about God's love and grace that takes my breath away. I am thankful that my life began with grace. Plenty of grace was needed on my journey; however, the grace of God and the grace of my parents set the stage. It is my prayer that I always live a grace-filled life full of God's love and peace.

APPENDIX 1

This, I Believe: Scripture References

- God the Father. Genesis 2:7, Psalm 103:13-14, Psalm 3:5-6, Psalm 138:8, Psalm 18:2, Psalm 139, Numbers 11, Exodus 3:7-10, Exodus 3:13-14, Psalm 90:2, Isaiah 43:10-11, Job 38-42, Psalm 100:3, Psalm 68:19, 1 Peter 2:9-10, Isaiah 6:3, Isaiah 25:1, Romans 8:29-30, Jeremiah 33:3, Psalm 145, 1 John 1:5, Lamentations 3:23, Genesis 1:26-27, Psalm 107:1

- God the Son. Genesis 1:26, John 1:1-5, John 1:14, Luke 1:34-35, 2 Corinthians 5:14-15, 2 Corinthians 5:21, Luke 4:38-40, John 11:5, John 14-17, Romans 5:8-9, Isaiah 53:4-6, 1 Peter 2:24, John 19:30, Matthew 28:1-10, 1 Corinthians 15:6, Luke 24:50-53, Romans 8:34, Mark 13:32, John 14:6, Colossians 1:15-17, Philippians 2:6-11, Hebrews 1:3

- God the Holy Spirit. Genesis 1:2, Genesis 1:26, John 14:15-27, Ephesians 1:13, Ephesians 1:19, John 16:5-15, Romans 8:1-17, Romans 8:11, Romans 15:13, Luke 24:49, Acts 1:8, 2 Corinthians 12:9, 1 Corinthians 12, Romans 12:6-8, Galatians 5:16-26, Acts 5:3-4

- Trinity. Genesis 1:26, Deuteronomy 6:4, Matthew 28:19, John 10:30, John 14:10, John 14:16,26

- The Bible is God's living and breathing Word. Deuteronomy 4:1-2, Psalm 19:7-10, Psalm 119, Hebrews 4:12, 2 Timothy 2:14-17, Romans 15:4, Romans 16:25-27, Hebrews 1:1-2, 2 Peter 1:21, Colossians 3:16

- Man is sinful and without hope apart from God's redeeming work. Genesis 1:26, Romans 3;23, Romans 6:23, James 2:10, Romans 8:1, 1 John 1:9, John 14:6

- Salvation is a free gift and the only way to move from spiritual death to spiritual life. Romans 6:23, John 3:16, John 6:44, Romans 10:9-13, Acts 3:19, John 14:6, Ephesians 2:8-9

- The Church is made up of God's people. Acts 2:42-47, 1 Corinthians 1:2, 1 Corinthians 3:16, 1 Thessalonians 2:8, Colossians 1:18, 1 Corinthians 12:14-30, 2 Corinthians 11:2, Hebrews 10:19-25, Luke 12:35-48, Matthew 28:18-20. The book of Acts tells the story of the development of the early church. The Pauline epistles and the general epistles were written to specific churches and leaders.

- The mission of the Church is to take the gospel of Jesus Christ to every tongue, tribe, and nation. Isaiah 6:1-8, Acts 1:8, Romans 10:14-15, Revelation 7:9-10, John 13:35, 2 Corinthians 2:14-15, Matthew 9:36-38

- Our daily goal is to conform to the image of Jesus. 1 Thessalonians 4:1, John 17:17, 1 Thessalonians 5:23, Romans 8:28-29, John 8:31-32, 1 John 2:28, Ephesians 5:1

- We glorify God when spiritual fruit is produced in and through our lives. Isaiah 32:17, 2 Peter 1:3-4, Ephesians 2:10, John 15:1-8, 1 Peter 3:15

- We are never alone. Exodus 15:13, Psalm 91, Romans 12:2, 1 Corinthians 1:9, Philippians 4:5, Acts 23:11, Isaiah 48:17, Isaiah 25:1, Galatians 5:1, Hebrews 4:16, John 10:10, Jeremiah 29:11, 1 John 3:10, 1 John 4:10, Romans 5:8, 1 Corinthians 1:9, Romans 8:37-39, Deuteronomy 31:6, Hebrews 13:5-6

- Diversity is a beautiful thing and should be celebrated. Revelation 7:9-12, Revelation 21:1-7

ABOUT THE AUTHOR

Andrea Lennon

Andrea fills many different roles. She is an "on the go" kind of girl who loves Jesus and shares His message of hope with those she meets. From washing ball uniforms to speaking at women's ministry events, Andrea embraces life and looks daily for opportunities to grow in her relationship with Jesus.

As the founder of True Vine Ministry, her passion is to encourage women to know the truth, live the truth, and share the truth. Through speaking and writing, Andrea enthusiastically shares the teachings found in the Bible and helps women apply the Bible to the everyday aspects of life. (Like how to stop yelling at the kids and kicking the dog!)

Andrea is a 2004 graduate of Southwestern Baptist Theological Seminary. She has written and published Reflecting His Glory: From Conformity to Transformation, Free To Thrive: 40 Power-packed Devotions for Women on the Go, and On the Road with Ruth. She has released two teaching DVDs that complement her Bible studies and books. Andrea hosts a weekly radio program called Truth on the Go with Andrea Lennon. She also serves as the Women's Ministry Specialist for the Arkansas Baptist State Convention.

Andrea and her husband, Jay, live in Conway, Arkansas, with their two sons, Jake and Andrew. Andrea travels extensively and thanks God for the opportunities to meet women, hear their stories, and teach the Bible.

To learn more about Andrea and True Vine Ministry, visit her website at www.andrealennonministry.org.

More Publications from
True Vine Ministry!

REFLECTING HIS GLORY

From Conformity To Transformation

Reflecting His Glory: From Conformity to Transformation explores Romans 12:2. This study provides a step-by-step approach for you if you long to:

- Recognize conformity in your life

- Understand the call to spiritual transformation

- Establish a daily process for renewal

- View God's will from His holy perspective, not your own.

Join Andrea Lennon as she leads you to discover life-changing truths that teach you how to think like Jesus, act like Jesus, and ultimately reflect Jesus Christ. Come away from this study changed, living for God's glory and not your own.

FREE TO THRIVE

40 Power Packed Devotions for Women on the Go!

In *Free To Thrive* author Andrea Lennon presents a clear biblical picture of freedom through 40 power-packed devotions. Each devotion invites you to know and experience God's freedom in every area of your life.

Free to Thrive topics include:

- Embracing God's definition of freedom

- Viewing sin through the eyes of a holy God

- Heeding the words of Christ

- Basing your life on correct theology

- Fighting a constant fight

- Doing whatever the Lord asks you to do

- Passing the point of no return

- Longing for your real home

ON THE ROAD WITH RUTH

Faith for the Journey

Ruth stood on the road between Moab and Bethlehem and considered two very different lives. A life that had been and a life that could be. The choice she made echoes down to our age. Ruth's story is riveting because it is full of heartbreak, loss, and soul-deep restoration.

Daily we stand in the middle of our roads and make decisions that shape our lives. No matter the road that we face, we can know that God is in control and that He has a plan for our lives.

In this book, Andrea shares the story of Ruth. Along the way, she encourages you to examine your own story. Come along on this journey and discover how you can live a life that honors God through:

• Embracing the right set of beliefs

• Displaying Christ-like character qualities

• Living with an eternal perspective during uncertain times.

54245617R00185

Made in the USA
Columbia, SC
27 March 2019